When Kids Are Apathetic

Jay Kesler
Ben Sharpton

David C. Cook Publishing Co. Elgin, Illinois—Weston, Ontario

First Aid for Youth Groups
When Kids Are Apathetic

Published by
David C. Cook Publishing Co.
850 N. Grove Ave., Elgin, IL 60120
Cable address: DCCOOK
Illustrations by Bill Duca
Design by Randy Maid
Printed in U.S.A.

ISBN: 1-55513-511-0

FirstAid FOR YOUTH GROUPS

When Kids Are Apathetic

About the Authors

Jay Kesler is president of Taylor University in Upland, Indiana. He has worked with youth for more than 30 years, much of that time as president of Youth for Christ. He is also the author of several books, including *Parents and Children* and *Parents and Teenagers* (Victor).

Jay wrote the "Battling Apathy" article for this book.

Ben Sharpton has been actively involved in youth ministry for over 15 years. An experienced creator of youth programming for such series as *Hot Topics Youth Electives* (David C. Cook), he works as a writer in Florida.

Ben wrote sessions 1-15 of this book.

Does Your Group Need First Aid?

Wise is the youth worker who heeds this rule: "Expect the unexpected."

Whether they're as intensely personal as an eating disorder or as far away as a famine . . . whether they're as "minor" as a question about rock music or as devastating as a suicide . . . problems, questions, attitudes, and crises will arise that disrupt the life of your group.

Is it really possible to prepare for such disruptions? Now it is—with "First Aid for Youth Groups."

Each book in the "First Aid for Youth Groups" series is designed to help you respond quickly to specific issues, situations, and events that affect your group.

With the practical, biblical advice contained in each session, you'll be able to help your group members handle and learn from such crises as an accident or natural disaster, a terminal illness, or a teen's pregnancy. You'll be ready to respond to group members' questions as to whether a Christian can be gay or why God could allow good people to go to hell. You'll be prepared to address specific reasons for group apathy or immaturity. And you'll be able to help group members deal with such personal hurts as sexual abuse and physical impairment.

Created with the help of veteran youth workers, these sessions do more than address the problems and crises affecting individuals in your group. They're also designed to raise the sensitivity of other group members, and to cause the group itself to be an instrument of healing.

No one can solve serious problems with a meeting or two. But with "First Aid for Youth Groups," you can be ready with immediate help when symptoms appear. The prescription: Pick sessions as needed and apply the wisdom of God's Word directly to your group.

— Randy Southern, Series Editor

Battling Apathy

Teenagers care only about themselves. They complain that youth meetings are boring; they claim they don't have time to read the Bible; they refuse to show up because their friends won't be there. They're more concerned about wearing the right clothes than about real *problems in the world. They're superficial, unconcerned, and apathetic about church, youth group, their relationships with God, and the world at large.*

You've heard similar complaints about today's teenagers. You may even have voiced a few yourself. You're not alone. In any analysis of the current youth culture the word *apathy* appears near the top of the list.

What's causing this epidemic of apathy?

Some say today's teenagers have gone back to the future—recalling the carefree and unconcerned youth of the Eisenhower era. Though the symptoms of seeming self-preoccupation and lack of concern for others are similar, their causes are very different.

Much of the apathy of 1950s teenagers stemmed from ignorance about the world's problems. With plenty of consumer goods and a strong economy, the America of the '50s was a secure, self-sufficient, isolated island. That's not the case today.

Due to instant communications and a shrinking globe, today's young people are not apathetic out of ignorance. In fact, many do care deeply about the world, their families, and vital issues of life and death, right and wrong. But unlike youth of former generations, they feel *they* don't matter. When television graphically delivers news of bloody conflicts or starving children, when newspaper headlines shout about gang wars and random violence, when the pastor preaches the plight of unsaved millions, today's teenager asks, "What could I possibly do about all this?" Young people suffer from an identity crisis, a feeling of smallness in the midst of overwhelming challenges.

In the past, the parents and grandparents of your young people dealt with issues that hit close to home. They had to help support the family or care for younger siblings and older relatives. Their contributions were concrete. But today's issues are often systemic, global, and catastrophic. As a result, teenagers feel powerless, and the only way they feel they can cope is to withdraw. When they are criticized as apathetic and selfish, it is not the result of self-preoccupation of a surface nature, but rather a deeply rooted struggle for competence and significance.

The situation has been echoed in the church. In the past, young people were part of the church body; there were no separate youth groups or youth ministries. Today the church may unwittingly contribute to teenagers' apathy. When the "adults" run the programs, young people are left on the sidelines—relegated to their own group of peers. Often ministry is done *to* them instead of *with* them. This also contributes to the feeling of helplessness that leads to apathy.

I believe that ultimately the solution is only available through a biblical understanding of the nature of the world and the role of human beings. The world as we experience it without God is indeed a planet out of control. As Christian adults it is our task to help youth see the world as *God's* creation. The world is not like a pinball machine on "tilt" with all of the lights blinking randomly. God will consummate the age and will bring all confusion, rebellion, chaos, injustice, pain, and inequity to a just resolution.

And God does not expect us to solve the world's problems alone. He has promised, "Never will I leave you; never will I forsake you." As we help youth to gain a Christian and biblical world view and lead them into a personal commitment to Jesus Christ, they become aware that they are not alone. Because they are a creation of a powerful and caring God, they can participate with Him in making a difference in the body of Christ as well as the larger world.

There is only one truth in this universe that can ultimately rescue modern man from the identity crisis. That is the fact that the God who created the universe is actually concerned for each of us as individuals. And He has demonstrated and proved that interest and commitment by visiting our planet and dying on the cross for our personal sins as well as for the sins of the whole world. People who criticize the simple Gospel and seek mega-solutions on their own overlook the profound central truth of Christ's coming. He came to save us from our aloneness and insignificance so we can join Him in His plans to redeem this fallen and desperate world.

As teachers and youth workers we are faced with the challenge of communicating this central Gospel truth which, when understood and appreciated by a young person, is absolutely life-transforming. We then are faced with the task of helping them to take on the challenges of their world in appropriate bite-sized pieces. Not only do we have to break the problems down to a workable size, but afterward we must go with them and assist them through the challenges of dealing with those problems.

This book can help you do that in some very practical ways. Its sessions tackle a variety of problem areas where your young people might be displaying apathy. Each session employs creative application of biblical principles and is interesting enough to reach even the most bored teenager.

Ultimately, apathetic youth must be allowed to make a difference. Churches that sponsor mission trips, do group clean-up and building projects, take food to the hungry, assist the poor, expose youth to diversity, plan stress camps, and employ simulation games, case studies, and creative programs beyond classroom teaching are making a significant impact on young lives caught up in this tragic loss of self-esteem. The Gospel is the key to the turnaround. God bless you as you embark on this most important and rewarding effort!

— Jay Kesler

Session 1

You've got a lot of competition for your kids' time and mental energy: television, movies, friends, athletic activities, homework and, probably your stiffest competitor, a kid's imagination. If you lose his attention for more than 20 seconds, he kicks into fantasy mode.

But you've got a lot going for you. First, your group is designed to help kids grow in faith, undeniably one of the most important tasks in life. Second, your kids can participate in making their youth group what they want. This places the responsibility for its interest on both of you. Third, they can make suggestions to make their meetings more interesting. That's where you use the individual's imagination to your advantage. Let them fantasize. Encourage them to dream. Have some fun together. Then kids won't say . . .

"This Group Is Boring"

Specific Aims

• To help kids recognize that the primary purpose of the group is to facilitate Christian growth; to help them understand that the group is what they make it; and to provide a forum for them to offer suggestions on how to make the group more exciting.

Scriptural Support

• John 6:63; 8:31, 32; 10:10
• Romans 12:2-8
• Philippians 4:8, 9

Special Preparation

• Bibles
• Copies of Student Sheet 1-A ("According to . . .")
• Copies of Student Sheet 1-B ("Let's Get Specific")
• Pencils
• Chalkboard and chalk or newsprint and marker

1 Boring Memories

Divide your group into pairs. Give each person a chance to share the following things with his or her partner, one at a time. Encourage each pair to search for similarities.

Tell your partner about:

- **The last time you were "bored to death."**
- **The most boring class you've ever taken in school.**
- **The most boring movie or TV program you've ever watched.**
- **One activity that always bores you.**
- **The most boring event you've participated in at church.**

You might choose to ask three or four volunteers to share their answers to one of the above boring incidents with the rest of the group. Next, ask each person to share his or her answers to the following:

Tell your partner about:

- **The last time you were really "fired up and excited."**
- **The most interesting class you've ever taken in school.**
- **The most interesting movie or TV program you've ever watched.**
- **One activity that never bores you.**
- **The most exciting activity you've ever participated in at church.**

Give three or four volunteers a chance to share their answers with the rest of the group.

Finally, ask each person to tell the group one positive thing about his or her partner that is *not* boring.

2 Chairman of the Bored

Bring everyone back together and explain that the group is going to examine several activities in an effort to determine which are most boring. Ask group members to say the word "boring" if the activity you read is one that bores them. If they feel the activity is *really* boring, they should say "boring" more loudly. If they think the activity is *really, really* boring, they should stand up and shout the word "boring!" If, on the other hand, they don't consider the activity to be boring, they should remain quiet.

The activities are as follows:

Algebra (math) class
Football game
Evening news
Classical music concert
English class
Astronomy
Playing golf
Watching someone else play golf
Sunday school
Worship service
"Mr. Rogers"
Missionary slide show
Nursing home visitation
Family reunion
History class
Politics

Documentary films	**Nintendo**
MTV	**This group**

Ask: **What is boredom?** Write two or three definitions on the board. (You might get answers such as, "Having nothing to do"; "Doing the same old thing"; "Being uninterested in people, activities, or events.")

Is boredom really the same as having nothing to do? (Not necessarily. We can have a long list of things to do, yet not be motivated to accomplish them.)

Point out that some people turn to TV, radio, or the movies when they get bored. Ask: **Can entertainment always relieve boredom?** (No. We have more opportunities for entertainment than any other group of people in all of history, yet we still get bored.)

In your opinion, what causes something to be boring? (Repetition; doing things alone; doing things that aren't challenging, etc.)

What can prevent something from being boring? (Staying on the edge of something new; participating with a variety of people; trying to see things from different perspectives, etc.)

Can an activity be both challenging and boring? (Probably not. By its nature, a challenge is not boring.)

Hand out copies of Student Sheet 1-A ("According to . . ."). This exercise asks each person to determine what eight different people (or characters) would say about your group. Give group members time to complete the exercise. Then ask them to form small groups of four (with their partners and another pair from the first activity) and share their responses.

After group members have shared their responses, ask them to rate the boredom level of the group on a scale of 1-10 (10 is "Exciting!" and 1 is "Zzzzzz"). Have groups determine their average response by adding the numbers and dividing by four—the number of people in the group. Ask each small group to share its average ranking aloud. Add up the rankings and determine the average ranking for the entire group.

Point out that later you'll be looking at ways to improve your group's score. But first you want to see how Scripture offers a prescription for the "Boredom Blahs."

3 Battling the Boredom Blahs

Write the headings of the following chart on the board. Divide your group into five small groups and assign each one of the following passages of Scripture. (If your group is small, divide into fewer groups and assign more than one passage to the groups.)

Group 1—John 6:63
Group 2—John 8:31, 32
Group 3—John 10:10
Group 4—Romans 12:2
Group 5—Philippians 4:8, 9

Each group should examine its passage and fill in the answers to each question on the chart. Once the chart has been filled out, give groups a chance to explain their answers. The following chart is filled in with answers to supplement your group members' responses.

Passage	What's Offered in This Passage?	What's Required in This Passage?	How Can This Help Overcome Boredom?
John 6:63	God's life-giving Spirit	Obedience to Jesus' words	God's Spirit makes life complete and full.
John 8:31, 32	Truth	Obedience to Jesus' teaching	You will be set free.
John 10:10	Life in all its fullness	Follow Jesus	Life in its fullness is exciting.
Romans 12:2	Knowledge of the will of God	Let God transform you inwardly by renewal of your mind.	Knowledge of God's will can give us fulfilling lives.
Philippians 4:8, 9	God's peace with you	Fill your mind with godly things.	God's peace isn't boring.

Ask: **How is "life in all its fullness" or "abundant life" the opposite of boredom?** (The abundant life is full of challenges and opportunities.)

How can Jesus "set us free" from boredom? (His challenges can give us a new enthusiasm for life; knowing Jesus deepens our experience of life.)

The Romans passage talks about a "mental transformation." Are the activities of this youth group a part of that mental transformation process? (They can be.)

4 Boredom Brainstorm

Brainstorm together and list all of the things that you do in this group. Write this list on the board. Your list might include Bible study, sharing, service projects, games, singing, and more. Divide the group into the five small groups from the previous activity. Ask small groups to examine each of the activities that your group does in light of their definition for boredom. (If you have numerous activities, assign a few to each group).

Ask: **Which activities tend to be boring?** Place a check mark beside these activities.

Which activities are no longer relevant or useful? How can they be adapted to be more relevant or useful? Should any be dropped completely—or for a brief period?

What can be done to make the activities of this group more challenging and interesting? (Young people can be more involved, particularly since the activities of the group are a part of the transforming process mentioned in the Romans passage. Perhaps additional adult leaders can help "spice up" the activities. Other activities or another setting can help make group meetings more exciting.)

How much should you be responsible for keeping our activities from becoming boring?

What specific things can you do to reduce or relieve boredom? (Participate actively; avoid being judgmental about others' answers; offer suggestions; pray for the leadership, etc.)

5 Get Specific

Pass out copies of Student Sheet 1-B ("Let's Get Specific"). Ask group members to take time to fill out the questionnaire, indicating things that they think would make the youth group more interesting and things they would be willing to do to help. After group members have completed their surveys, ask them to sign their forms. Each should then ask a friend to witness his or her signature.

Bring everyone together for a closing worship moment. Sing an appropriate song, and ask someone to read Romans 12:3-8. Then share the following prayer together:

Heavenly Father,

We want this youth group to be an exciting, inspiring, and supportive group. We want the activities to be memorable and the topics to affect our lives. We want You to meet us here and we want to introduce You to our friends. Take our talents and use them. Take our thoughts and direct them. Take our lips and speak through them. Amen.

Collect the forms and use them in your next planning meeting to identify areas and activities that need to be changed. You might also create an index card file or computer database containing this information for future use.

According to . . .

1-A

Try to imagine how the following people might feel about your youth group. What words would each use to describe your activities, meetings, discussions, etc.? Write a brief sentence or two beside each name.

Your parents "   ."

The most popular kid in your school "   ."

Your pastor "   ."

Your favorite movie star "   ."

____

Your best friend "   ."

The President of the United States "   ."

A popular rock star "   ."

____

You "   ."

Now, on a scale of 1-10 (10 = Exciting! and 1 = Zzzzzz) rate your youth group (circle one):

Zzzzzzzz								Exciting!	
1	2	3	4	5	6	7	8	9	10

LET'S GET SPECIFIC

Take a close look at each of the following things that might take place in a youth group. As we work together to make this group exciting and interesting, which activities would you like to participate in? Which would you be willing to help lead? Place a check mark by all that apply.

PARTICIPATE	*LEAD*	*ACTIVITY*
❑	❑	Discussions of important topics
❑	❑	Bible study
❑	❑	Group prayer time
❑	❑	Games/recreation
❑	❑	Service projects/outreach programs
❑	❑	Spiritual retreats, camps, etc.
❑	❑	Fun trips to amusement parks
❑	❑	Snacks/meal preparation for youth group
❑	❑	Group singing
❑	❑	Creative worship—speaking, Scripture reading, etc.
❑	❑	Singing in quartets, trios, solos, etc.
❑	❑	Multi-media presentations (slide shows, video, etc.)
❑	❑	Operate sound system when necessary
❑	❑	Photography
❑	❑	Interpretive movement
❑	❑	Creative drama (skits, plays, etc.)
❑	❑	Puppetry
❑	❑	Clown ministry
❑	❑	Youth newsletter/publicity
❑	❑	Church newsletter/publicity
❑	❑	Telephone calling to publicize events
❑	❑	Inviting other young people to the group
❑	❑	Visiting members of the church who are sick
❑	❑	Other ______________________

Now, sign this form indicating your commitment to participate and lead as indicated above. Ask another member of the group to witness your signature by signing his or her name under yours. The witness should hold you accountable for what you've said you will do.

Signed, ______________________

Witnessed by ______________________

Session 2

Let's face it. No matter how hard you try or how likable you are, some young people just won't get along with you. There will be disagreements and personality conflicts. Many kids (just like adults) find they relate to one adult better than another. That's a strong motivation for building a *team* of adults to work with your youth group.

When kids don't seem to like you, often the only thing you can do is to continue to love them and continue to be yourself. Sometimes, however, the opportunity will come along when kids feel they can offer positive suggestions about how you can lead them. Take advantage of these times, evaluate their feedback, and work to make your ministry as effective as you can.

"I Don't Like the Leader"

Specific Aims

• To help kids understand the sacrifice, work, and care that go into leading a group of teens; to help them understand their biblical responsibility to respect the leader; and, in a sensitive, nonthreatening manner, to give them an opportunity to provide helpful feedback to the leader.

Scriptural Support

• Romans 15:1, 2; 16:17, 18
• I Corinthians 1:10
• I Peter 5:2-7

Special Preparation

• Bibles
• Copies of Student Sheet 2-A ("Personal Strength Checklist")
• Copies of Student Sheet 2-B ("Positive Feedback Form Letter")
• Pencils
• Chalkboard and chalk or newsprint and markers
• Several boxes of toothpicks

1 Personal Check-up

As group members arrive, hand out copies of Student Sheet 2-A ("Personal Strength Checklist"). Ask each person to evaluate his or her own strengths, using the checklist.

After everyone has had a chance to complete the student sheet, divide your group into small groups. Explain that group members are now going to have the chance to affirm one another. Each small group should start with the person in that group who has lived in your community the longest. Other members of the group should name strengths from the "Personal Strength Checklist" which they have seen in that individual's life. After group members have identified three or four items, they should move to the individual's right and identify the strengths in the next person's life.

When everyone has had the opportunity to be affirmed, ask: **How did it feel to be affirmed by the group in this way? Was it difficult to affirm others? Were you surprised by some of the strengths others said you had?** (Group members may discover that it's sometimes more difficult to be positive than negative. It can be embarrassing to be on the giving or receiving end of affirmation. We sometimes find it easier to see weaknesses than strengths—even in ourselves.)

2 Leader Check-up

Introduce the topic for this session by saying something like: **During this session we're going to change things a little bit. We often talk about ways you can improve this youth group or ways you can grow in your faith. Now let's talk about ways *I*** (or *we,* if several adults lead the group) **can improve the youth group. It might be hard to do, but I want you to be honest and candid with me, and offer some true feedback on strengths and weaknesses of this group's leadership.**

Ask everyone to examine his or her "Personal Strength Checklist" again and evaluate the strengths of the adult leader of the group (you). If there is more than one adult leader, group members should select the leader that they have the hardest time getting along with (no need to mention names). To evaluate a leader, each person should place a check in the boxes on the right side of the page beside the strengths held by the leader.

Ask: **How does the leader match up to your own checklist? Did any of the strengths of the leader surprise you?**

Divide the group into the small groups from the previous activity. Ask each group to brainstorm together and write down characteristics that the *ideal* adult youth leader might possess (such as strong knowledge of the Bible, time for kids, lots of patience, and a powerful prayer life). After the groups have created their lists, ask individuals to share three or four of these characteristics with the rest of the groups. During this time, each group might choose to add new characteristics to its list.

Give each group a box of toothpicks. Ask each person to think of one adult youth leader, but not to reveal who that person is. Have a volunteer in each group read the characteristics of ideal youth leaders one at a time. If the leader that a young person chose possesses that characteristic, the young person should place one toothpick in the center of the group. For example, if the leader Mary was thinking about was very patient, Mary would place a toothpick in the circle when that characteristic was read. If Julie was thinking of another person (or even the same person) who was also patient, Julie would also place a toothpick in the center of the circle. By the end of this activity, each group should have a lot of toothpicks in the center of the circle.

Then ask groups to brainstorm again, and list things they dislike about typical adult leaders (such as being unprepared, being too strict, playing favorites, etc.). Invite them to do the same ranking process with these characteristics. As one person reads from the list of negative characteristics, each person should *remove* a toothpick from the center of the group if the characteristic applies to the leader about whom he or she has been thinking.

After the evaluation process, ask the following questions: **What did you learn about your adult leader(s)? What surprised you? Are any toothpicks left over for your group? What does this say about your leader(s)? What does this say about you?**

3 Respectfully Yours

Keep your group in the same small groups used in the previous activity. Ask someone in each group to read Romans 15:1, 2 and I Peter 5:2-7.

Then ask each group to come up with its best definition of "respect" based on these passages. Have each group write its definition on the board.

Ask each group to create a list of suggested guidelines for adult youth leaders from these passages of Scripture. (Some examples might include: help carry the burdens of the weak; don't work to please yourself; build up others in Christ; be an example for the followers; humble yourself.)

Invite volunteers to share their guidelines with the rest of the group. Ask each group to look at the passages again and to create a list of suggested guidelines for group members. (They will probably discover that most of the same guidelines created for adults apply to young people.)

Ask: **How would following these biblical guidelines help us respect each other?** (By following them, we put the needs of the other person first. That can lead to mutual respect, as we often have to respect others before they will respect us.)

What keeps us from respecting each other? (Lack of understanding; putting ourselves first; feeling our needs have been overlooked; personality conflicts, etc.)

What keeps us from respecting our leaders? (The same problems that keep us from respecting each other.)

4 Divide and Conquer

Before the session, ask two volunteers to be argumentative during this activity in order to "divide the group." No matter what they believe or what the group says, they should always pick the *last answer.*

Tell the group that you are going to ask several multiple choice questions to identify strengths of the group. You will ask group members to raise their hands to show how they would answer each question. After each question, ask group members to comment on why they voted as they did.

1. **What are the best things about this youth group?**
   a) The people who attend
   b) The activities the group does
   c) The snacks the group eats
   d) The Bible studies
2. **What made you come to this youth group initially?**
   a) One of the adults invited me
   b) My parents
   c) I wanted to attend one of the activities (Offer specific example.)
   d) A friend invited me
3. **What are the worst things this group does?**
   a) The Bible studies
   b) Service projects
   c) Games
   d) Nothing
4. **What are you most proud of that this group did over the last year?** (Offer four examples.)
   a) ___________________________
   b) ___________________________
   c) ___________________________
   d) ___________________________
5. **This group is . . .**
   a) Very tight (close)
   b) Divided
   c) OK
   d) I don't know

Ask the two volunteers for this activity to read Romans 16:17, 18 and I Corinthians 1:10. Ask: **How can divisions hurt our group?** (They can create hurt feelings and limit spiritual growth.) **What do we do that is divisive?** (We sometimes criticize others just to build ourselves up.)

Point out that the two volunteers were helping in this activity, and were trying to divide the group. Ask: **How did you feel about their behavior? How did they affect the group?** (Some might have felt threatened or irritated at the actions of the volunteers.)

Explain that disagreement is OK as long as it doesn't become personal or lead to divisions. It's important to be honest about our negative feelings and lovingly (and privately) confront those we disagree with.

5 Case Study Conflict

Tell group members that now is their chance to show what they would do as youth leaders in some sticky situations. Divide them into three small groups. Share one of the following situations with each group and ask each to recommend the best way to handle that situation. Give each group time to share its answers with the rest of the group.

Case #1

For some reason, Lisa never has gotten along with the youth leader. It may have started at the first meeting she attended. The leader, in an effort to be funny, said something that offended Lisa. At any rate, she refuses to attend the youth group as long as "The Jerk" is in charge. You like Lisa, and you tolerate (even appreciate) "The Jerk." You think both of them could contribute something important to the group. What do you say to Lisa? Do you say anything to "The Jer—" er, the leader?

Case #2

Mrs. Smith has come to see the youth leader. It seems her daughter refuses to attend the youth group. "Julie says she . . . doesn't like you," Mrs. Smith explains. What should the youth leader say to Mrs. Smith? What should Mrs. Smith do? What responsibility does Julie have? Would it make a difference if Mrs. Smith were the pastor's wife?

Case #3

Kevin used to be very active in your group, but he has started going to the church down the street. They have a new youth director who surfs, plays all kinds of sports, and is funny. Kevin says it's a better group; he says he gets more out of the meetings and feels more at home. The problem is that Kevin used to be one of the most active members of your group. Now that he's gone, things just don't seem the same. You would like him to come back and help your group (and its leader). What do you say to him?

6 Letter Have It!

Pass out copies of Student Sheet 2-B ("Positive Feedback Form Letter"). Invite each person to write a letter to his or her adult leader(s) by completing the form and leaving it in the room. The letter offers an opportunity to express hopes and dreams about the youth group. Remind kids to use the back if they need more room.

Close in prayer, thanking God for the privilege of working with this group. Invite others to add their own sentences to the prayer before you say, "Amen."

Personal Strength Checklist

Place a check mark in the box at the left to identify any personal strengths you believe you possess. Leave the boxes on the right blank until you are asked to do otherwise.

ME	*STRENGTHS*	*LEADER*
❑	Always attends the activities of this youth group.	❑
❑	Makes an effort to listen to others when they speak.	❑
❑	Shows concern for each member of this youth group.	❑
❑	Shows love for God.	❑
❑	Demonstrates compassion for those less fortunate.	❑
❑	Makes time for people in this group.	❑
❑	Tries to be a spiritual vessel which God can fill.	❑
❑	Prays for the members of this youth group regularly.	❑
❑	Knows the Bible well.	❑
❑	Fun to be around.	❑
❑	Builds up other members of this group.	❑
❑	Goes the “extra mile” for members of this group.	❑
❑	The group would miss this person if he or she were absent.	❑
❑	Deeply respected by members of this group.	❑
❑	Other ______________________________	❑
❑	Other ______________________________	❑
❑	Other ______________________________	❑

POSITIVE FEEDBACK FORM LETTER

Fill in the blank spaces on this form letter to share your thoughts with your youth leader. Give the letter to him or her at the end of this session.

____
(Youth Leader's Name)

____
(Youth Group's Name)

____
(Church's Name)

Dear ____________________________:
(Youth Leader's Nickname)

Thank you for

____

____

I wanted you to know that I respect

____

____

One thing that bothers me about the group is

____

____

Another thing that bothers me about the group is

____

____

In the future, I'm going to make a strong effort to support you by

____

____

Sincerely,

____
(Your name)

Session 3

The world today can be a frightening place. Wars, death, injustice, disasters—all compete for newspaper headlines and television air time. How could any teenager *not* care about what's happening?

Yet some of your group members seem to tune out the world's bad news. They act like only *their* problems are important.

Though such self-preoccupation is typical of their age group, it's important for young people to look beyond their immediate situations. Their fears or feelings of helplessness shouldn't stand in the way of concern for hurting people in our world.

You can help them step outside the small circle of their lives and practice compassion. When they see they can make a difference, they might find that the world isn't such a frightening place after all.

"I Don't Care What's Going On in the Rest of the World"

Specific Aims

• To give kids a graphic idea of just how many hurting people there are in the world; to help them understand that they have the ability to make a difference in these hurting lives; and to help them recognize the example Jesus set for us in relating to hurting people.

Scriptural Support

- Luke 10:25-37
- John 12:24-26

Special Preparation

- Bibles
- Copies of Student Sheet 3-A ("Current Events Pop Quiz")
- Copies of Student Sheet 3-B ("Parable of the Good Atheist")
- Pencils
- Chalkboard and chalk or newsprint and marker
- Eight flashlights
- Materials to "lightproof" the meeting place

1 What's Important to You?

Write the following list on the board:
Your belongings
Your self-worth
Your friends
Your freedom
Your home
Your education
Your money
Your clothes
Your family
Your faith
Your planet
Your happiness

Divide the group into small groups of three. Ask each person to rank the items listed above in order of their importance (from most to least important). Give each person a chance to discuss his or her five most important rankings with the rest of his or her small group. Bring everyone back together in a large circle and ask: **What similarities did you find in your group? What big differences exist? Did any rankings surprise you?**

Say something like: **You might feel the most important things in life are those that directly affect you—in concrete, visible ways. But what about world events and needs that aren't so close at hand? How do the headlines make a difference in your life? And how can *you* make a difference in the issues that grab headlines? Let's start by seeing how familiar you are with major issues and events of the past few years.**

2 Current Events Pop Quiz

Hand out copies of the Student Sheet 3-A ("Current Events Pop Quiz"). Explain that this is an anonymous quiz, and that group members should not sign their names. Give each person time to complete his or her quiz. Have kids grade their quizzes using the answers from the following key.

(1) f. 1,000
(2) e. 11,000,000
(3) b. 67
(4) c. 8,000,000,000
(5) g. 29
(6) d. 47
(7) h. 200,000
(8) i. 462
(9) a. 3,300,000,000,000
(10) j. 7,300,000

Ask everyone to determine the grade for his or her quiz by giving each correct answer 10 points. Each should write his or her total grade in large numbers at the top of the page. Collect quizzes. Have a volunteer add all the grades and divide by the number of quizzes to determine the average grade for the group. Also, ask the volunteer to total up the responses for question #11.

Explain that you will get back to the quiz results later.

3 En-lightening Experience

Have group members sit in a circle. Evenly distribute seven flashlights around the circle. Keep one flashlight for your own use. (If you have fewer than seven participants in this group, give everyone a flashlight and double up on some of the directions below.) Ask each person who's holding a flashlight to turn it on. Turn off the room lights.

Say something like: **Right now we're going to examine some of the things that have happened in our world in the last several years. You might ask yourself, why even bother talking about things that happen in Africa, or Beirut, or Australia? After all, those things are way over on the other side of the world. The answer is quite simple. In today's world, we're all affected by whatever happens, even in the most remote countries.**

For example: (Ask light person #1 to turn off his or her flashlight.) **Three black people are killed in a riot in South Africa, and people in the United States start a boycott against companies that do business in South Africa.**

(Ask light person #2 to turn off his or her flashlight.) **Iraq invades Kuwait and gas prices skyrocket. The stock market responds by plummeting. Prices go up everywhere, and the country's recession deepens.**

(Ask light person #3 to turn off his or her flashlight.) **Hundreds of Chinese students are murdered for their protests against an oppressive government, and the world is much further from being free.**

(Ask light person #4 to turn off his or her flashlight.) **Developers destroy forests in Central America, and thousands of species of animals and plants (some of which may have proven to be biologically beneficial in the treatment of various diseases) are destroyed with them. The rest of the world is in danger because that region produces much of the oxygen in our world.**

(Ask light person #5 to turn off his or her flashlight.) **An eleven-year-old boy in Belfast admits that he would like to join the Irish Republican Army to "Kill Orangemen and Brits." He adds, "But I wouldn't kill one of my own." And he thinks his behavior is in line with his religious beliefs.**

(Ask light person #6 to turn off his or her flashlight.) **A devout Christian lady dies in her apartment in Chicago because she can't afford heat. She's donated her life savings to a television evangelist.**

(Ask light person #7 to turn off his or her flashlight.) **Iraq, before giving up its occupation of Kuwait, almost completely destroys the country, leaving behind billions of dollars in damage and environmental devastation.**

At this point you may want to turn off your flashlight—the last light remaining. Use your judgment on what kind of effect this will have on the mood of your group. You may decide to leave it on so that "crowd control" won't be sacrificed.

Now ask individuals to suggest words or phrases that describe how they feel. (In the dark; alone; depressed, etc.). Ask how members of your group feel when so much seems to happen in their world in such a short period of time. (Frightened; out of control, etc.) Ask: **Is it easier to ignore the things going on than to face them? Why or why not?**

Say something like: **The bad news is the world can be a dark place of pain, fear, and loss. The good news is that God is in control and He has put us here to be light by helping one another.**

(Ask light person #1 to turn on his or her flashlight.) **A massive hurricane strikes the East Coast and your church rushes donated supplies (including some of your old clothes) to the aid of the disaster victims.**

(Ask light person #2 to turn on his or her flashlight.) **Enough East German citizens speak out against a repressive regime and the Berlin Wall tumbles to the ground.**

(Ask light person #3 to turn on his or her flashlight.) **A high school football player commits his life to Christ at a Fellowship of Christian Athletes conference after hearing a college football player's testimony.**

(Ask light person #4 to turn on his or her flashlight.) **A group of hostages is released from a Middle East country. One of them is from your hometown.**

(Ask light person #5 to turn on his or her flashlight.) **A pastor's daughter attends a college in Gainesville, Florida. News reports tell of five brutal murders in the college community in three days. In less than five hours, she receives two invitations to stay with the families of two other pastors who live in the city.**

(Ask light person #6 to turn on his or her flashlight.) **Your best friend's father has a nervous breakdown and becomes abusive toward her and her mother. They find shelter in a safe-house set up and supported by a group of churches in your town. After much persuasion, her father seeks professional counseling through an organization of Christian counselors.**

(Ask light person #7 to turn on his or her flashlight.) Mention one of the service projects your youth group or church has participated in and how that has helped "bring light into the world."

Now ask individuals to suggest words or phrases that describe how they feel. (Hopeful; positive; grateful, etc.). Ask: **Is it possible, in this age, to survive as an isolated people?** (No. We're all connected.) **In what ways are we connected with people all over the world?** (Through our beliefs, our economies, our shared resources.)

4 Who Is My Neighbor?

Ask a volunteer to read Luke 10:25-29. Say something like: **In Jesus' time—just like today—the world was full of divisions. People stuck to their own groups and were reluctant to reach out and help others. The question, "Who is my neighbor" is as important to us today as it was when Jesus answered it with the Parable of the Good Samaritan. Let's take a look at that parable in its origi-**

nal version, and in one that's slightly updated.

Ask a volunteer to read Luke 10:30-37. Then recruit eight volunteers to participate in a reader's theater based on this parable (double up on parts if your group is small).

Pass out copies of Student Sheet 3-B ("Parable of the Good Atheist") and make assignments. (For fun you might want to assign guys the roles of girls and girls the roles of guys.) Encourage actors to "ham it up" as they perform the play.

5 How Do We Rate?

Ask your volunteer scorekeeper to share the average grade that your group made on the Current Events Pop Quiz. Ask: **What does this tell you about our group?** (Discuss whether your group seems to be well-informed, not only concerning the quiz, but on issues in today's headlines.)

Ask volunteers to share their responses to question #11 (how concerned they are about their world). Say something like: **Jesus taught us to care for our neighbors, which includes anyone in need. What keeps us from doing that?** (Too busy; don't know how, etc.)

6 I Really Don't Care

Ask: **What things might happen around the world if Christians didn't care so much about comfort, power, money, etc.?**

Ask someone to read John 12:24-26. Ask: **What does God want according to this passage?** (In following Jesus' example, we should give from our own resources to help others.)

Suggest group members look once again at the list of valued things from Step 1. Challenge them to reorder some of their priorities in light of today's session.

Close with the following prayer: **Father, help us to stop caring about the things that don't really matter, about the comforts and luxuries of life. Instead, help us to seek out, help, and care about our neighbor whoever and wherever he or she might be. Help us to lose ourselves in You that we might find ourselves in You. In Jesus' name. Amen.**

CURRENT EVENTS POP QUIZ

Match the numbers below with their descriptions. (Place the corresponding letter in the blank to the left of the description.)

a. 3,300,000,000,000	d. 47	g. 29	j. 7,300,000
b. 67	e. 11,000,000	h. 200,000	
c. 8,000,000,000	f. 1,000	i. 462	

_____ 1. The number of students who were ambushed for their support of democracy in Tiananmen Square, Beijing, China on June 4, 1989 (according to Amnesty International).*

_____ 2. The number of gallons of oil that spilled into Prince William Sound, killing thousands of wild animals after the *Exxon Valdez* ran aground.*

_____ 3. The number of people who died in the San Francisco earthquake on October 17, 1989.*

_____ 4. The cost, in dollars, of Hurricane Hugo's five-day attack on Charleston, South Carolina, the Virgin Islands, and Puerto Rico.*

_____ 5. The number of years the Berlin Wall separated East and West Berlin.*

_____ 6. Percentage of black children living below the poverty line in the U.S.**

_____ 7. The number of children in the world under the age of 15 who are soldiers, according to the United Nations.***

_____ 8. Number of gang murders in Los Angeles in 1988.***

_____ 9. The 1990 national debt, in dollars.

_____ 10. The number of American families who lived in poverty in 1986.****

_____ 11. (Extra credit) I am:
a. Very concerned about the world in which I live.
b. Kind of concerned about the world in which I live.
c. Not really concerned about the world in which I live.
d. Not at all concerned about the world in which I live.

* *Time* magazine, June 4, 1990
** *The Harper's Index Book*, 1987, *Harper's* magazine
*** *Time* magazine, June 18, 1990
**** "Tracking Tomorrow's Trends," *USA Today*, 1986

Parable of the Good Atheist

CAST
Narrator
Man
Bad Guy #1
Bad Guy #2
TV Evangelist
Churchgoing Lady
Atheist
Hospital Receptionist

NARRATOR: Once a man opened the front door of his house, and went for a walk. It's really not that uncommon. People do it every day. While he was on his walk, some bad guys saw him coming.

BAD GUY #1: Look. That man's going for a walk.

BAD GUY #2: Ya wanna mug him, take all his money, and run off?

BAD GUY #1: Sounds like a good plan to me.

BAD GUY #2: Let's do it!

NARRATOR: So they mugged the man, took his money, and ran off. The man lay dying on the side of the road.

MAN: Oooooh. Ooooooooh, I'm dying.

NARRATOR: A TV evangelist was driving along that road on his way to a finance meeting.

EVANGELIST: Oh, my. There's a poor, unfortunate wretch lying beside the road, and it looks like he's dying. I wish I could help, but we have that important finance meeting, and a fifteen-million-dollar budget. I'll just drive on.

NARRATOR: Then a churchgoing lady rode by on her bicycle.

LADY: My goodness, look ahead. It's someone who's hurt and dying alongside the road. Oh, what can I do? I know, I'll be sure to pray for him as soon as I get to church.

NARRATOR: Then an atheist passed by.

ATHEIST: Oh, no. Someone's hurt. I've gotta help him.

NARRATOR: The atheist picked the man up and carried him to the local hospital.

ATHEIST: Here's some cash to take care of him. If his bills are higher than that . . .

RECEPTIONIST: They probably will be.

ATHEIST: I'll pay the rest when I get back.

NARRATOR: Now, in your opinion, which of these people acted most like a neighbor?

ALL: The guy who was kind.

NARRATOR: Then you do the same thing. The end.

Session 4

Does it ever seem that your group members have a two-part faith? Part one came when they were younger; they were "saved." For many that meant a guaranteed escape from eternal punishment and a promise of heaven somewhere down the road. Part two comes later—living the Christian life with Jesus as Lord when they're older, married, settled down. Right now these young people are in spiritual limbo between part one and part two. Their lives look much the same as the lives of their non-Christian friends. It's important to challenge them to step out of this limbo and into a *real* Christian life.

Unfortunately, young people often think of a Christian lifestyle as a life full of "thou shalt nots," when, in reality, the life that Christ promised is abundant. This session might be an ideal time to explain that Jesus came to offer life in all its fullness. Such life is worth living at any age.

"I'll Worry about Living for Jesus When I'm Old"

Specific Aims

- To help kids recognize the folly of expecting to live to a certain age; and to help them recognize that a young person can serve Jesus just as effectively as an older person can.

Scriptural Support

- Luke 12:16-21
- Philippians 4:8, 9
- Colossians 2:6, 7

Special Preparation

- Bibles
- Copies of Student Sheet 4-A ("By the Time I'm . . .")
- Copies of Student Sheet 4-B ("Philippians Picture Charades")
- Pencils
- A piece of candy (or fruit) for each participant

1 Long-Term Goal Setting

Ask each person to share his or her response to the following question: **What is one thing that you want to accomplish in your life?** (Have a happy family; be successful in business; have a college education; travel, etc.)

Pass out copies of Student Sheet 4-A ("By the Time I'm . . ."). Explain that this is a tool for thinking ahead—for setting some long-term goals. Give everyone a few minutes to complete the questionnaire.

Break into small groups to share answers. Start with the oldest person in each group and ask that person to share what he or she would like to have accomplished by the age of 21 (the first fill-in-the-blank statement on the student sheet). Move to the first person's right and ask the next person to share his or her answer. Continue until all group members have told their groups their responses. Then examine responses for the second item in the same fashion. Continue until all of the statements from the questionnaire have been shared. Ask group members to hang on to their student sheets for a later activity.

To introduce the session, say something like: **We all have personal goals that we want to accomplish in our lives. One of mine is ___________. Some people believe that a relationship with God is an integral part of life and dreams. Others decide to keep God out of the picture until later in life so He doesn't get in the way of their dreams and goals. During this session, we want to talk about both of these approaches to life.**

Let's start by examining two different perspectives—for and against Christian ideals and beliefs.

2 Pro and Con

Divide your group in half. Assign half the kids the role of being "Pro," or for Christian ideals. Ask the other half of the group to take the role of "Con," or against Christian beliefs. Explain that you are going to ask the group for typical responses to Christian issues. No matter what group members actually believe, during this activity they should try to think as someone who is for or against Christianity, depending upon the group they are in. For example, if you ask, "What do you think about tithing?" members of the Pro group might say, "Tithing is a way to express our thanks for what God has done," or, "We give a tenth of our earnings to help minister to others." Members from the Con group might say, "Tithing is just another way for the church to get richer," or, "It's a waste of money."

This activity should help kids focus on the promises of God and on understanding how non-Christians view Christians.

ISSUES		POTENTIAL RESPONSES
What is a Christian?	PRO	(Someone who believes in Jesus as Lord.) (Someone who trusts God to forgive his or her sins.) (A person who is born again.)
	CON	(Someone trying to relieve his or her guilt through religion.) (Someone who still believes in his or her parents' religion.) (A wimp.)
What do you think about television evangelists?	PRO	(They're trying to lead lost souls to Christ.) (They're doing God's will.)
	CON	(They take advantage of the poor, elderly, and weak.) (They're phonies.)
What does a relationship with Christ offer you?	PRO	(Eternal life.) (Exciting, fulfilling life.) (Peace and assurance.)
	CON	(A guilt trip.) (A life as boring as you are.) (People just like yourself.)
Why do people become Christians?	PRO	(To keep from going to hell.) (Because their friends are Christians.) (To make the fullest possible expression of their beliefs in God.)
	CON	(They're afraid to face reality.) (Because nobody else will accept them.)
Why do people attend church?	PRO	(To worship God.) (To learn and grow in faith.) (For fun!)
	CON	(To put on a show for others.) (To relieve their guilt.) (Habit.)

Conclude this activity with a statement like: **You'll probably agree that there are good and bad reasons for doing the things Christians do. Because we all have the freedom to behave as we wish, we can choose how we will live our lives.**

3 A Taste of the Good Life

Pass out candy (or fruit) to each person. Ask each to refrain from eating it. Remind everyone that the question you're dealing with in this session is, "Why shouldn't I wait until I'm older to live for Jesus?"

Say something like: **One view is that we should get the best stuff out of life as soon as we can—kind of like eating your candy** (or fruit) **right now, instead of waiting until later.** Ask if everyone agrees. Ask volunteers to suggest what sort of things a person who was waiting to become a Christian would want to do (drinking, cheating, premarital sex, stealing, etc.).

In a way, the Christian view is exactly the same. Christians believe that we should get the best stuff out of life as soon as we can. In fact, the sooner, the better. Just like eating your candy (or fruit) **right now. The difference is in how we define "the best stuff in life."** Ask volunteers to suggest the things that a Christian would say are the best things in life (caring, loving relationships, peace of mind, a balance of work and play, etc.).

Invite everyone to eat his or her candy (or fruit) now.

Move on to the next section by saying: **One question we need to ask is, "Is the Christian way of life so bad?" Let's look for a moment at Paul's description of ideal Christian behavior.**

4 The Best Worst-Case Scenario

Ask a volunteer to read Philippians 4:8, 9. Pass out copies of Student Sheet 4-B ("Philippians Picture Charades"). Have group members pair off. Working quickly, each should fill in the squares with illustrations of the traits listed in Philippians 4:8, 9. (For example, to illustrate "things that are true" one might draw a picture of the Bible. The hard part is that no written words are allowed!) The partners should try to guess what is being drawn. After five minutes, have the partners switch so the other person can draw.

Bring everyone back together in a large group. Ask a volunteer to read the passage again. Use the following questions to help participants get a clear understanding of it.

What do you think of the guidelines that Paul recommended for Philippian Christians?

Point out that they are worthy behaviors, regardless of a person's faith.

Tell me what the opposite of these traits are:

Things that are excellent. (Things that are bad.)

Things that deserve praise. (Things that deserve condemnation.)

Things that are true. (Things that are lies.)

Things that are noble. (Things that are vulgar.)

Things that are pure. (Things that are polluted.)

Things that are lovely. (Things that are ugly.)

Things that are admirable. (Things that are shameful.)

What if, just for speculation, there were no afterlife? Let's say I commit my life to Christ, live a worthy life as outlined in this passage, and die and face the same fate as a non-Christian. Didn't I still live a better life, full of good, positive experiences? The Christian life makes sense.

5 The Worst Best-Case Scenario

Ask everyone to take another look at Student Sheet 4-A ("By the Time I'm . . ."). Ask someone to read Luke 12:16-21. Ask volunteers to sum up this passage in single sentences: The moral of this passage is . . . (Live for yourself and you might have nothing but yourself to live with. You can't be sure what tomorrow may bring. God has something better than the best you can plan for yourself.)

Work backwards through the student sheet, comparing kids' personal dreams with the promise of eternal life. You might say something like: **What if you don't live until you're 65 and never get what you've identified as a goal for that age? Won't you have more with a relationship with God? What if you don't reach your 60th birthday? Aren't the Christian promises still worth your commitment? What if you don't live to be 50?** Continue through the list.

6 Case Study Challenge

Divide your group into three small groups. Assign each group one of the following situations. Challenge each group to come up with its best response, based on the passages of Scripture discussed during this session. Then give each small group a chance to share its case and its response with the whole group.

Case #1

You used to be good friends with Sam. His parents are active in your church. Sam used to be. Recently, however, he's dropped out. He's cultivating a new crowd of friends, and you seldom see him anymore. You worry about him, and you miss him. After all, you had a lot of fun together!

You happen to run into Sam in the hall at school. You invite him to your next youth activity: a weekend retreat to a favorite campground. Sam just shakes his head, disinterested. "Church is fine for you," he says. "I'm going to wait until I'm older to get serious about Jesus." What do you say?

Case #2

You met Sherry at summer camp two years ago. You haven't seen her since then, but you write each other every now and then. Lately her letters have seemed to change. She's got a new boyfriend and never writes about the kids in her youth group anymore. In your last letter you got a bit bold and asked her what had caused the change. Her response: "I just don't have the time for that anymore. It seems like a whole lifetime away." What do you do? If you write her back, what will you say?

Case #3

Your older sister got married four years ago. She and her husband stopped attending church shortly after they became engaged. They said they were just too busy. Last year she had her first child. Now they're back at church every Sunday. They attend all the family events and are even thinking about teaching a Sunday school class.

You're curious about the change. You ask your sister to explain what happened. What do you think she'll say?

7 Personal Responses

Ask two or three volunteers to share why they've chosen to become Christians now, instead of waiting until they're older. (It's a good idea to ask these people ahead of time to prepare to share.)

As a closing prayer, ask someone to read Colossians 2:6, 7.

By the Time I'm . . .

Fill in the following blanks to show what you hope to accomplish by the time you reach that age. (To spur your thinking, check out the list of possibilities at the bottom of this sheet.)

By the time I'm 21, I will

____

By the time I'm 25, I will

____

By the time I'm 30, I will

____

By the time I'm 40, I will

____

By the time I'm 50, I will

____

By the time I'm 60, I will

____

By the time I'm 65, I will

____

Possibilities

be happily married
have written a book
own my own house
own my own car
own stocks
have traveled around the world
have had grandchildren
have been featured in a *People* magazine article
own a boat
own my own business
have a child
have two or more children
have graduated from college
have completed grad school
have a doctoral degree
be financially independent
have met my favorite movie star

Philippians Picture Charades

Fill in each square with a specific illustration of something in the category listed. (For instance, you could draw a picture of a Bible under "things that are true.") Remember, you can't use any written words, signs, or symbols.

Things that are good

Things that deserve praise

Things that are true

Things that are noble

Things that are pure

Things that are lovely

Things that are honorable

Session 5

Friends are important, especially to teenagers. You're probably not surprised to learn that one of the main reasons your kids attend your group is to see their friends. That's OK. Right now most young people put friendship higher on the priority list than spiritual growth. But is there some way you can motivate them to take more personal responsibility for their commitment to the group? Now's the time to help them analyze just why they are part of your group and understand the importance of their participation.

And what about the kids whose friends don't attend your group? They may not hang around much longer unless they make some new friends in your group—or invite their current friends. Here's help in challenging them to do just that.

"I'll Show Up Only If My Friends Do"

Specific Aims

• To give group members the motivation to become spiritual leaders among their peers and take the initiative to invite their friends to church and youth group meetings.

Scriptural Support

• Luke 5:27-32
• John 1:35-42; 3:22-30; 4:7-30
• Colossians 4:2-6

Special Preparation

• Bibles
• Copies of Student Sheet 5-A ("Friendship Survey")
• Copies of Student Sheet 5-B ("A Note from Gary")
• Pencils
• Children's building blocks
• A garden hose or a strong rope

1 The Unbroken Circle

Attach the two ends of a garden hose together (or tie a rope together tightly) so that it forms one large circle. (For smaller groups, you may need to double the hose several times to decrease the dimension of the circle.) Ask everyone to grab a portion of the hose and to walk backward slowly. When the hose becomes taut, ask everyone to stand still.

Explain that the circle represents your youth group. The circle has no beginning and no end, like God's love. It connects the members of the group to each other, as God's Spirit does. If everyone were to lean back, the circle (the hose) would support them. Ask group members to slowly lean back, letting the hose hold them up. Say something like: **What would happen if someone dropped out of this group?** Ask one person to let go of the hose (or rope). The group will have to respond to take up the slack.

Ask: **What if several of this person's friends decided not to come because he or she didn't come anymore?** Ask three or four people from the same side of the circle to let go of the hose and watch how the group has to compensate to take up the slack.

Ask volunteers to share insights on this brief exercise. (We need each other; if we drop out just because our friends do, others who depend on us will be hurt.)

2 What Would We Do without You?

Tell group members that you're glad they attend your group because it just wouldn't be the same without each person there. Offer an example. (For instance, "If Jimmy weren't a part of this group, my canoe wouldn't have turned over on the last retreat, and it wouldn't have been as much fun," or, "If Anne weren't here, we wouldn't have as many great backrubs in this youth group.")

Now give everyone a chance to affirm others about similar traits and events. Divide your group into small groups. Let group members share one thing about each person in their group that they would miss if that person weren't a part of your group. After everyone has had an opportunity to affirm and be affirmed, ask: **How do you feel right now?** (Needed; important; cared for, etc.) **Why don't you always feel that way in this group?** (People sometimes forget to show they care; we get caught up in other things, etc.)

3 Lean, Mean Voting Machine

Examine some of the ingredients of your youth group to determine what is most important to the members of your group. Explain that you're going to ask them to vote for things that they really like and things that they really don't like about the group. You will name several activities that the group has participated in or ingredients that make up the group, one at a time. After each item, group members should show how they felt about that item by leaning to the right if they liked the item and to the left if they didn't care for it. If they have neutral feelings, they should stand still.

The items are as follows:

- Last week's meeting
- Your last overnight event
- Your last group trip
- The people in this youth group
- Sunday morning worship services
- Singing hymns during Sunday morning worship services
- Singing during youth group meetings
- The captivating, engrossing, exciting Bible studies this group shares
- The recreation that this group does
- Sunday school
- Family activities at your church.

(Add as many specific activities as you can that your group has shared, such as lock-ins, retreats, meals, musicals, concerts, camping trips, mystery trips, mission events, etc.)

Ask: **What single ingredient is the most important to you in this youth group?** (Most will probably identify friends as the most important ingredient.) **If that one ingredient were taken away, would you still benefit from the activities of this group?** (Most will probably say the group would still be beneficial, but not as much.) **Would you participate if we did away with that ingredient?** (Most would probably say, "Yes, but not as often.")

Ask for volunteers to share who had the greatest impact on their being at this meeting (a youth leader, a parent, one of the group members, etc.) Give time for several people to share.

Say something like: **Friends make up one of the most important ingredients of this youth group. They're important. If your friends weren't here, it's possible that you might not be here either. And that's not good because you would miss out on all the fun and spiritual growth activities this group offers.**

4 Friendship Checklist

Pass out pencils and copies of Student Sheet 5-A ("Friendship Survey"). Ask everyone to complete the worksheet by writing in names of at least five friends and by following the directions at the bottom of the page. This activity will help group members examine the interactions they have had with their friends. Explain that these worksheets will be confidential; no one will see what anyone else writes.

After everyone has completed his or her worksheet, ask for a show of hands to indicate how many people listed at least one friend who does not attend your youth group. Ask how many people listed two friends who don't attend the group. How many listed more than two names of people who don't attend this group? Ask volunteers to share how they feel about those friends who don't attend the group (They miss them; they sometimes feel left out, etc.).

Find out if any group members wrote down the name of someone else in the group who invited them to attend your group. Ask: **How would you feel if that person didn't attend this group anymore? Would that be enough to make you stop coming? How would you feel if that person only attended the "fun" activities?**

5 Four Responses to God

Divide your group into four teams. Assign each team one of the following passages of Scripture. Ask the teams to study their passages to determine:

- who the central character was;
- what his situation was;
- what Jesus (or God) did;
- how the individual responded to Jesus (or God).

Team A—Luke 5:27-32 (Levi was called to follow Jesus and responded by inviting his friends over to meet Jesus.)

Team B—John 1:35-42 (Jesus invited Andrew and others to follow Him and Andrew invited his brother, Simon.)

Team C—John 3:22-30 (John's disciples asked him who Jesus was and John encouraged them to follow Him. John added that Jesus should increase in importance and John should become less important.)

Team D—John 4:7-30 (Jesus spoke to a woman most Jews despised and told her about her sinful life. She left and told everyone that Jesus was the Messiah.)

Ask: **What is the natural response when someone meets Jesus?** (To share Him with friends.) **Why is this tough?** (We may be rejected; they might not understand; they might laugh at us.) **Why is it important?** (They need to know Jesus and we need to share our relationship with Him.)

6 A Note from Gary

Say: **Let's look at a hypothetical situation in which someone doesn't attend the group because his friends don't.**

Divide into the four teams from the last activity. Pass out copies of Student Sheet 5-B ("A Note from Gary"). Give each team a chance to read Gary's note and then to illustrate what team members would say to their friend, Gary.

One team will simply write a note back to Gary, describing what it thinks he should do. The second team will create a sculpture using Legos (or building blocks) that symbolizes what might happen if Gary (or others like Gary) only attended activities when his friends did. The third team should create a roleplay between two members of the youth group and Gary, depicting what team members might say to Gary should they have that opportunity. The fourth team should create a list of the "Ten Best Reasons to Attend This Group," which team members would naturally share with Gary if they had the chance.

Give each team an opportunity to share its responses with the other teams. Ask: **Why is it so tough to participate in activities when our closest friends don't? How can you help someone like Gary decide to become involved in our group?** (We can accept Gary when he attends; we can keep on inviting him; we can let him know that we understand how he feels.)

Why is it important to try to help people like Gary fit into a group like ours? (He needs a relationship with Jesus and we need the experience of sharing that relationship with him.)

Ask someone to read Colossians 4:2-6. Ask group members to think about the following questions. (They should not answer these questions aloud, but should think quietly about their answers.)

Would you drop out of this group if your friends didn't come?

Would you drop out of this group if we stopped doing fun stuff?

Would you drop out of this group if we changed adult leaders?

Would you drop out of this group if we stopped (one of the favorite activities that your group does)**?**

Do you attend this group only when your friends do?

How do you act toward unbelievers?

Do you make use of every opportunity to help them believe?

Do you give the right answers to their questions?

Have a volunteer read Colossians 4:2-6 again as a closing prayer.

Friendship Survey

5-A

Write down the names of five friends (people you usually speak to at least once a day) on the blank spaces below. These friends may or may not be involved in this youth group.

My Friends:

____

____

____

____

____

Follow these directions for each friend you identified above.

- Place a check mark (√) to the left of those people who attend your youth group.

- Did any of these people invite you to attend this group or class? Place a plus mark (+) to the left of those names.

- Did you ever invite any of these people to attend your youth group? Place a check mark (√) to the right of those names.

- Which of these people would really enjoy the activities of this group? Circle those names.

- Focus on the people on your list who normally attend your youth group. If any of them dropped out of the group, would their absence make you consider dropping out of the group as well? If so, underline their names.

A Note from Gary

Hi!

I'm in World History right now, and I thought I'd do something constructive. So, I'm writing a note to you.

Thanks for the invitation to attend your camping trip this weekend. Sounds fun. But . . .

I don't know. My friends don't go to church, and I guess we'll go catch a movie or something. I don't know many people who'll be on the trip. If Jeff or Karen were going, well . . . maybe.

You know, last winter that ski trip was a lot of fun. Jeff and Karen were there. Even Kyle made it to that one.

Well, you know what I mean. But thanks for asking.

Gary

Session 6

Someone has accurately said, "Your life may be the only Bible that another person might read." All we do in life—the way we behave, the decisions we make and the examples we offer—portrays to others our faith.

If our faith is alive, meaningful, and personal, it will affect the way we live. It will make a difference in virtually all that we do. If that faith is not well, then our lives will be divided into two distinct areas: the church and everything else.

But in both situations, we are still witnessing. Either our witness says, "My faith is of the utmost importance to me," or "Other things are more important to me than my relationship with God." You can help your group members evaluate which message they are communicating through their lives.

"I Don't Want to Make a Fool of Myself by Witnessing or Inviting Friends"

Specific Aims

• To help kids recognize the urgency of sharing their faith—that it's a matter of eternal life and death; to help them see that their fears of looking foolish pale in comparison; and to help them brainstorm practical methods of sharing their faith.

Scriptural Support

• Matthew 5:14-16; 28:19, 20
• Luke 10:2
• John 15:8
• I Corinthians 3:18-23
• Philippians 2:12-16
• I John 4:19-21

Special Preparation

• Bibles
• Copies of Student Sheet 6-A ("I Am an Island")
• Copies of Student Sheet 6-B ("What Would You Say?")
• Pencils
• A flashlight (or candle, light bulb, or other light source)
• An object (rock, glass, paperweight, etc.) which you have accurately weighed before the meeting

1 Foolish Definitions

Divide group members into pairs. Explain that you're going to ask them to define the word, "foolish." However, each pair must come up with a definition it believes *someone else* might offer. Use the following guidelines:

Pair A: Define "foolish" from your parents' perspective.
Pair B: Define "foolish" from your best friend's perspective.
Pair C: Define "foolish" from your teachers' perspective.
Pair D: Define "foolish" from your pastor's perspective.
Pair E: Define "foolish" from your little brother or sister's perspective.
Pair F: Define "foolish" from your perspective.

Give pairs time to create their definitions; then ask one person from each pair to share the definition with the rest of the group. After everyone has had an opportunity to share, ask: **What are some other words that mean the same thing as "foolish?"** (Silly, childish, stupid, dumb, etc.)

Foolish is such a general word. What does someone mean when he or she says, "I don't want to appear foolish by witnessing or inviting my friends?" (The person is afraid he or she would feel embarrassed if he or she were to invite friends.)

How can being a Christian be embarrassing? (We can't help but be aware of stereotypes that portray Christians as judgmental, hung up on rules, or boring.)

How can being a Christian be something you're proud of? (When we have a realistic and sensible faith, others can see what a difference it makes in our lives.)

2 An Experiment in Witnessing

Show an object (rock, glass, paperweight, etc.) that you have weighed prior to the meeting. Give group members a chance to examine the object. Ask them to find others who agree with them about the correct weight. (For instance, people who believe the rock weighs 12 ounces, people who believe it's 13 ounces, etc.) Eventually you will have several small groups.

After everyone has chosen a group based on his or her belief about the weight of the object, give group members five minutes to try to "convert" other people to their group.

When five minutes are up, bring everyone back together and talk about the activity. Ask: **Did any of you change your mind about the weight of the object? If so, what made you change? Did anyone strongly refuse to change? Did any of you feel foolish as you tried to persuade others to agree with your belief?**

Point out the parallels between trying to convince a person about the rightness of one's belief in the weight of an object and trying to convince a person about the rightness of one's belief in God. It can be difficult to convince someone who has his or her mind made up—especially when both parties have little information to base their beliefs on.

Tell everyone what the actual weight of the object is.

3 Taking a Stand

Define eight points along the perimeter of the room. The first corner will be *area 1.* The middle of the wall will be *area 2.* The second corner will be *area 3.* The next wall will be *area 4.* Continue until all corners and walls of your room have received a number. Area 1 stands for "This is definitely me." Area 8 stands for "This is definitely not me." The other areas represent degrees of agreement between the two extremes.

Explain that you are going to read several statements, one at a time. After each statement, you want everyone to move to the area that best represents the extent of his or her agreement with that statement. At that point you'll ask volunteers to answer a few questions with the other people who chose that response to help them clarify their stand on that statement.

Statement 1: **Faith is something very personal to me, and something I'd rather not share with others.**

Questions: **How is faith personal? When does faith involve others?**

Statement 2: **I use my actions as my main witness for God.**

Questions: **How are actions a good means of witnessing? How are actions a poor means of witnessing? Can actions be a lazy way of avoiding having to explain your views?**

Statement: 3: **At times I feel guilty about not sharing my faith.**

Questions: **Why do you feel guilty? How can you resolve that guilt? Why don't you feel guilty? Do you think a little guilt might be beneficial?**

Statement 4: **I have non-Christian friends that I wish were Christians.**

Questions: **What have you done about that? What would you like to do about that?**

Statement 5: **I have led someone to Christ before.**

Question: **How does your answer make you feel?**

Ask for volunteers to describe how they decided to become followers of Jesus. Try to get them to explain who had the strongest impact on their decisions and what those people said or did to persuade them to become Christians.

4 Outreach Committees

Divide your group into four teams. Ask each team's members to imagine that they belong to an outreach committee for your church. Give each team one of the following passages of Scripture, and ask each to create a one-sentence statement explaining why a young person should witness to his or her friends based on that passage. Then have each team share its sentences with the rest of the group.

- Matthew 28:19, 20 (Jesus commands us to go into all the world.)
- Luke 10:2 (There are many people who need to hear the Gospel.)
- John 15:8 (We become disciples by bearing fruit.)
- I John 4:19-21 (We love others and share God's love because He first loved us.)

5 Sharing God's Light

Ask someone to read Matthew 5:14-16 aloud. Pass a flashlight (candle, light bulb, etc.) around the circle. Ask each person to share how a Christian is similar to that object. (Christians show the way to go; they have freedom to turn off or on; light gives off warmth and so do Christians, etc.)

Brainstorm together and name as many different types of lights as you can. (Stoplights, flashlights, fire light, strobe light, caution light, firefly light, searchlight, etc.) Divide into the four teams from the previous activity. Ask group members to describe the people sitting on either side of them as lights. (For example: Mary's like a caution light, because she cautions us when we're getting out of line; Joe's like a searchlight, because he's always looking for people he can help.)

Ask: **How did it feel to be affirmed in this way? Do you feel foolish?**

Did you ever think of yourself as the kind of light that was chosen for you?

Would you have chosen a different kind of light for yourself? If so, how do you feel about the light that was chosen for you?

Ask someone to read aloud Philippians 2:12-16 to close this activity.

6 I Am an Island

Pass out pencils and copies of Student Sheet 6-A ("I Am an Island"). Ask group members to chart their own spiritual journeys on this map, by following the footprints from one end of the island to the other and placing various items from the legend that symbolize different times in their journeys. For example, if a young person's family went through a divorce, he might draw in the swamp symbol at that point in his journey. If another person felt a recent retreat was a high point of her life, she might draw a mountain to symbolize that time in her life.

Give group members time to chart out their spiritual journeys. They should be sure to write in the names of individuals who had an influence on their spiritual lives along the path wherever their influence was felt.

Divide into the four teams used previously and ask each person to share his or her drawing with the rest of the team. Challenge team members to listen closely to each individual's story.

Ask everyone to study his or her chart carefully. Ask: **What if those individuals who made a difference in your life for Christ had not been there? How would your life be different?**

Do you think someone might write your name on his or her spiritual journey map someday? What if you don't make the effort to witness to that person? Will it make a difference?

7 Practice Witnessing

So many opportunities to share our faith come out of ordinary conversations. Ask seven volunteers to participate in three roleplays. (If your group is small, you may need to double up on parts or just do two of the roleplays.) Give copies of Student Sheet 6-B ("What Would You Say?") to the volunteers and assign the roles. After each situation is played out, ask for others to suggest what else might have been said to encourage the friend to consider a relationship with God.

Share the following story in your own words: **A businessman had been struggling with doubts about his faith. One night, while on a business trip, he sat alone in a restaurant. Suddenly, another man appeared in the nearby window. He had a small sign in his hands which said, "I am a fool for Christ. I Corinthians 3:18." The businessman hurried outside to talk with the man with the sign, but he had moved on. The businessman hurried back to his hotel room, found a Gideon Bible and read I Corinthians 3:18-23.** Ask someone to read this passage. **The incident made him evaluate his life and turn it over to Christ.**

Ask: **How is God's wisdom different from worldly wisdom?** (God's wisdom is based on God's priorities.) **How can being foolish be a positive witness for Christ?** (When we least expect it, it can affect others' lives.)

Ask group members to quietly bow their heads and think of one person close to them who might need an invitation to this youth group or a chance to raise some questions about God. Ask what it will take for them to be the light in their friend's life. Ask: **Are you afraid of being a "fool" for Christ?**

Close in silent prayer, asking God to help each young person reach out to his or her friend.

I Am an Island

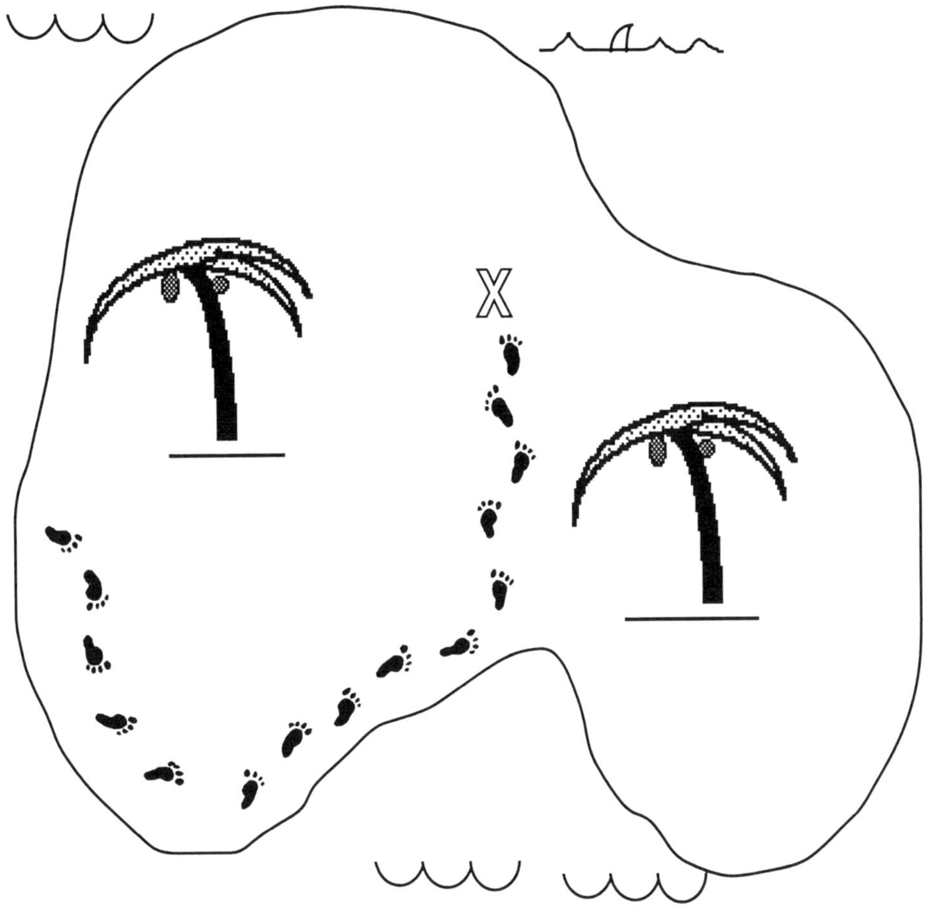

LEGEND

- Mountaintop Experience
- Swamp (Down time)
- X Marks the Spot (Now)
- Treasure (Value)
- † The Church

What Would You Say?

Roleplay #1

Tom is really troubled about his parents' relationship. They're always yelling at each other, and recently Tom's dad slapped his mother a couple of times. Tom wants to help them, but he doesn't know what to do or say. Deep inside, he wonders why God is allowing this to happen.

Roles: Tom
Karen (a close friend of Tom's, and a Christian)

Roleplay #2

Julie, Sherrie, and Kelly are riding in Julie's new red sports car. Julie has just invited some friends to her house for a swim. Hanging up her car phone, she begins describing how incredibly bored she is. She's looking for something that will inspire her and give her life real meaning.

Roles: Julie (a girl with just about everything)
Sherrie (a distant friend of Julie's and a new Christian)
Kelly (a close friend of Julie's and a Christian)

Roleplay #3

Larry has never felt accepted by anyone. He jokes that his parents moved around a lot when he was a kid, but he found them every time. He tells his one and only friend Jeff that he just can't seem to build good friendships. He always says the wrong thing and feels like an idiot.

Roles: Larry (a very lonely guy)
Jeff (Larry's only friend in the world)

Session 7

Kids have money. They receive allowances. One study in *Working Mother* magazine indicated that 90% of parents give an average of $8.13 in weekly allowances to their 16-year-old children. Another study estimated the average weekly allowance of a 13 to 15 year old to be about $14.00 per week. Teens 16 years old and older averaged $26.38 per week.

Kids also work. Polls indicate that 33% to 44% of teenagers work part time, earning an average of $26.80 (13 to 15 year olds) to $56.13 (16 to 19 year olds).

But having money and sharing it are two different things. In a self-indulgent world like ours, we need to encourage teenagers to share all that God has given them, including their wealth.

"I Have Better Things to Do with My Money Than Putting It in the Offering"

Specific Aim

- To help kids recognize that money is a gift from God, and that a portion of it should be given back to Him as a symbol of their commitment to Him; and to help them brainstorm creative ways they can put their money to use for God's work.

Scriptural Support

- Leviticus 27:30-34
- Luke 6:38; 19:2-8
- Acts 20:32-35
- II Corinthians 9:6-9
- I Timothy 6:17-19

Special Preparation

- Bibles
- Copies of Student Sheet 7-A ("Give Up?")
- Copies of Student Sheet 7-B ("Check Your Spending Pulse")
- Pencils
- Chalkboard and chalk or newsprint and marker
- Index cards
- Several boxes of toothpicks

1 Toothpick Trade-offs

Pass out about ten toothpicks to each person. Tell group members that you're going to play a game. During the first round, the object is for each person to get as many toothpicks as he or she can. There are only three rules:

• If someone asks you for a toothpick, and you have at least one, you have to give it to the person asking.

• If someone asks you for a toothpick, and you don't have any, that person has to give you one of his or hers.

• You can only give or receive one toothpick at a time.

Ask if anyone has any questions. If so, explain the rules once again. Begin the round and watch as everyone attempts to accumulate toothpicks.

After about three or four minutes of play, stop round one. Immediately, move into round two. In this round, the object is to give away all of your toothpicks. This time there are only two rules:

• If someone offers you a toothpick, you must take it.

• You can only give or receive one toothpick at a time.

Check to see if anyone has questions. Begin the round and challenge group members to give away all of their toothpicks.

After three or four minutes, call a halt to round two. Use the following questions to debrief:

Who received the most toothpicks and how did you feel?

Who didn't do so well?

How did you feel?

Was it difficult to ask other people for a toothpick?

What feelings did you experience during round two? Did anyone end up without any toothpicks? Was it difficult to give away toothpicks? Which was tougher, asking or receiving?

Point out in discussion that we often have mixed feelings about giving and receiving. We like to get things, but are sometimes too independent to ask. And we don't mind giving—as long as it doesn't really cost us too much. We know that we are supposed to be cheerful givers, but we don't always feel cheerful about sharing what we have.

2 Where Does All Your Money Go?

Pass out three index cards to each young person. Instruct group members to determine where they spend most of their money and write down the top three areas on the three cards (one on each card). While they are working, you may want to share the following information: **A Rand Youth Poll indicates that most younger teenagers spend their money on snacks, clothes, and entertainment. Older teens tend to spend their money on automotive products, clothes, and entertainment.**

Divide the group into small groups. Give each small group an equal number of cards. Ask the small groups to quickly place the cards in four categories: Vital, Important, Nice-to-Have, and Not Important.

Pass out four blank index cards to each group. Ask the groups to write one of the following items on each card:

- Something your church does to help people;
- Something else your church does to help people;
- The name of a charity or good cause;
- Another charity or good cause.

Then ask the groups to place these new cards in the categories they set up earlier. Chances are, most or all of these cards will be placed in the "Vital," or "Important" categories. Bring everyone back together in one large group and ask volunteers to share what they learned about how they spend or share their money.

Ask: **How do you feel about the three items on which you spend most of your money?** (Group members will likely see that the items on which they spend most of their money serve themselves instead of others. These items are not as important in the larger scheme.)

What would it take for you to spend more on things that can make a difference in the lives of others? (Some may want to have more personal involvement with giving, having more to say about where the money is going and how it will be used to help.)

3 Pick a Giver

Pass out copies of Student Sheet 7-A ("Give Up?"). This exercise presents descriptions of six "typical" students and, in a nonthreatening manner, lets kids choose one that is most like themselves, one that is most like the people in your group, and one that is most like the kids in their school. Give everyone time to fill out the worksheet.

After everyone has finished, ask volunteers to suggest which characters they chose that best describe the kids in their schools and the kids in their youth group. Then ask: **Which character would you most like to be like?** (You might choose to play "devil's advocate" and push them to explain their answers).

4 Principle Interest

Ask volunteers to tell you everything they remember that the Bible says about giving. (They'll probably say something like, "Tithe"; "It's more blessed to give than to receive"; "Give and it'll be given to you," etc.)

Draw everyone's attention to the board. Across the top write "Scripture," "Giver," and "Reason." Explain that you want the group to look at some examples of giving in Scripture. Assign the verses from the following chart to various individuals. Ask each to read his or her passage aloud. Then ask group members to determine who is (or should be) giving, and the reason for giving.

Scripture	*Giver*	*Reason*
Leviticus 27:30-34	The Israelites	Give because it belongs to God anyway.
Luke 6:38	God/Us	Give and God will give to you.
Luke 19:2-8	Zacchaeus	He gave out of gratitude, and to right the wrongs he had done.
Acts 20:32-35	Paul/Christians	You're happier when you give than when you receive.
II Corinthians 9:6-9	Christians	Be happy in giving because God supplies your needs.

5 A Message to the Rich

Ask: **Do you think of yourself as rich?** (Most will probably deny that they are. But compared to other societies, ours is extremely wealthy.) Explain that you are about to reveal what Paul suggested for people who are wealthy. You're going to read from I Timothy 6:17-19, but you want each person to listen to the passage from a different perspective. Ask those whose birthdays are from January through April to try to see what Paul's message says to wealthy *individuals.* Ask those born between the months of May and August to listen from the perspective of *poor people.* Ask the rest of the group to try to determine what Paul is saying to a *wealthy nation.*

Ask: **What did you hear Paul saying to your group? Is he condemning wealth?** (Apparently not. He's just suggesting that we place our values elsewhere.) **In what ways can we do good and share out of the riches God has given us?**

6 Supporting What's Important

Say something like: **Most information sources agree that teenagers spend a lot of money every year. In fact, kids in the U. S. will spend about $65 billion this year alone. Companies recognize that, and focus their advertisements on youth. Let's think about what might happen if Christian teenagers gave more to help others and spent less on themselves.**

As you work through this list of ideas, write on the board the amount of money that could be freed up to help others. After each "ballpark" figure, ask the group to suggest specific ideas for spending that money.

• You give up one soft drink every day. (Annual savings: $150)

• You take a part-time job (10 hours per week) and give the money to God's work. (Annual earnings: $1,200)

• You convince your family to eat one meatless meal each week, and give the savings to someone else. (You could feed hundreds in a lifetime.)

• You clean out your bedroom and hold a garage sale to raise money for charity. (It's almost beyond imagination.)

• You give $5 a week to the church and live to be 80 years old. (You would have donated $20,800 over your lifetime.)

Have group members brainstorm additional ways to save or raise money and suggest projects that could benefit by their gifts.

Ask someone to read I Timothy 6:17-19 as a closing prayer. Pass out copies of Student Sheet 7-B ("Check Your Spending Pulse"). This is a brief worksheet designed to help kids chart their spending for one week. Challenge them to track their spending closely for the next week.

Give Up?

Generous George

George gives 100%, 100% of the time. When he plays football, he plays harder than anyone else. When he studies, he's a librarian's dream. And when he gives or serves, he gives and serves *all*. In fact, he never has any money because he donates so much to charities. He never has any time to talk because he's always listening—to kids in the hospital, to a crisis hot line, or to his little brother or sister. In fact, it seems like George doesn't have anything. He's given it all away.

Sometimes Sally

Sally gives . . . sometimes. She helps out with youth group service projects on occasion. She drops some coins in the offering every now and then. She gives her own time to help others from time to time. The problem is, Sally is inconsistent. No one knows when to depend on her. Her church stopped sending her dated offering envelopes. Instead, it gave her a handful of blank ones and asked her to just fill in the date when she gets around to it.

Ted Tithe

Ted gives a tenth—of everything. He sets aside 10% of his allowance for the church. He schedules 10% of his time for prayer and service. He even gives 10% of his dinner to his dog (usually the broccoli and breadcrusts). But don't ask him for more than 10%, because he's already doing his "fair share."

Nancy Never

As hard as it might be to believe, Nancy would never give to anything or anybody. She hangs on to everything she's got—her time, money, material goods—and consequently, that's about all she's got. Not many people think of themselves as *her* friends.

Plan-Ahead Pete

Pete is the most organized guy in the world. He has a tighter schedule than *TV Guide*. His budget was designed by a professional accountant. Pete knows what he's going to give, and who he's going to give it to months in advance.

Level-Headed Larry

He tries to give. He makes a strong effort to know what his church is doing with his gifts. He gives not only money but also his prayers and his physical presence when possible. Sometimes he slips up, but most of the time, he reaches his goal of supporting his church with his time, talents, and gifts.

Which character are you most like? ______________________________

Which character are you least like? ______________________________

Which character would you like to be more like? _________________________

Which character would your pastor like you to be like? __________________

Which character would your parents like you to be like? __________________

Which character would God like you to be like? _________________________

Check Your Spending Pulse

Jesus said that your heart will be wherever you spend your money. So, where is your heart? To find out, jot down everything you purchase this week. At the end of the week, see for yourself. You might find it necessary to rearrange your spending habits to bring them in line with your values.

Purchase	Price
______________________	______
______________________	______
______________________	______
______________________	______
______________________	______
______________________	______
______________________	______
______________________	______
______________________	______
______________________	______
______________________	______
______________________	______
______________________	______
______________________	______
______________________	______
______________________	______
______________________	______

Session 8

Time. Everyone has the same amount, but nobody has enough of it. We all think we'd live better lives—work harder, grow spiritually, help others—if we only had more time. But in reality, lack of time is not the culprit. Our *priorities* determine how we spend our limited time resources. So the excuse, "I just don't have time," actually means, "I just choose to spend my time elsewhere." The kids who attend your group activities do so because they've chosen to make it a priority. It isn't a priority for kids who don't attend.

The key, then, is encouraging kids to make church and youth group activities a priority. Relationships are one way of achieving this. As kids build relationships with adult leaders, other kids in the group, and God, they make group activities a priority. Instilling the desire to grow in faith is another way of encouraging kids to make the group a priority. Setting a good example also helps.

During this session, challenge kids to make the group a priority and to examine their daily agendas to make room for the group regularly.

"I Just Don't Have Time"

Specific Aim

- To help kids recognize the importance of scheduling time for church involvement and making the group a priority; and to help them honestly assess their time priorities to see what could be rearranged to make time for the group.

Scriptural Support

- Exodus 18:13-27; 20:8-11
- Ecclesiastes 3:1-8
- Matthew 22:15-21
- Ephesians 5:15-17

Special Preparation

- Bibles
- Copies of Student Sheet 8-A ("Clock Work")
- Copies of Student Sheet 8-B ("Goal Mining")
- Pencils
- Chalkboard and chalk or newsprint and marker
- About ten index cards for each person
- About 25 beans (or tokens, pennies, or marbles) for each person

1 Just Like Clock Work

Divide the group into small groups. Pass out pencils and copies of Student Sheet 8-A ("Clock Work") to each person. This worksheet provides an affirmation exercise which also helps introduce the topic of time.

Each person should write the names of the other small group members beneath the clocks that most remind him or her of those people. Next, going around the circle, each person can affirm the others in the small group by explaining his or her choices and the reasons for them.

After allowing plenty of time for affirmation, say something like: **We are a society of clock-watchers. That's because time is precious to us and we hate to waste it. Let's think of different ways you could be spending your time right this minute.**

2 A "Things to Do" List

As a large group, brainstorm together and list on the board things that group members could be doing at this moment. (Watching a TV show; playing tennis or basketball; biking; talking on the phone; doing homework, etc.)

After you've created a large list, say something like: **With all of these things to occupy your time, why are you here?** Don't let them give easy answers, like, "I dunno," or "This is better." Press each volunteer to be specific about what attracts him or her to this group and why this group is a priority.

What are your friends who don't attend this group doing right now? Group members will probably read several popular activities off the list you just brainstormed.

Why do they choose those things over the youth group? Try not to make group members defensive. Don't blame them for the people who aren't present.

3 Time for Everything

Ask someone to read aloud Ecclesiastes 3:1-8. Ask: **What do you think? Is there a time for *everything*? How do you decide which activity should be in a time slot?** ("Put God and His work first"; "It all comes out right in the end"; "Strive for a balance.")

Divide into small groups used previously. Pass out about ten index cards to each person. Say something like: **We're going to try to map out our priorities. On each card write down one activity that is important to you.** (Suggest things such as school, family activities, sporting events, clubs, hobbies, church activities, etc.). After group members have written one activity on each card, have them place the cards on the table or floor in front of them in order of most important to least important. Invite kids to share their priorities with their small groups.

Pass out about 25 beans (or tokens, pennies, etc.) to each young person. Ask group members to think about the 10 activities on their cards. They should place one or more beans on each card to symbolize how much time they spend on that activity each week. (For instance, John writes the activity, "playing the piano" on his card. He only plays about 30 minutes a week—not much compared to other things that occupy his time—so he places 1 bean on the "piano" card. Another important activity is John's job, which takes 15 hours per week. John places 5 beans on the "job" card.)

Invite everyone to move around his or her small group and closely examine the cards and "bean placement" in that group. Ask: **If you didn't know the people in your group as you do, but you saw the way they spend their time, what observations would you make about them? What would you say are the most important priorities in your group? Is amount of time a good indication of priorities?**

4 Ordering Priorities

Say something like: **We've all been given the same amount of time in a day. You have 24 hours and I have 24 hours, every day. When someone says, "I just don't have time," isn't he or she really saying, "I've got other things that are occupying my time"? So what we're really talking about is where to place our priorities. Let's see what Scripture says about that.**

Give each group one of the following Scripture passages. Ask each group to study the passage and summarize what it says about our use of time and setting priorities:

- Exodus 18:13-27 (Jethro tells Moses to delegate responsibilities so he can better use the time he has.)
- Exodus 20:8-11 (Honor the Sabbath and keep it holy. Dedicate one day each week to God.)
- Matthew 22:15-21 (Give to Caesar—that is, the government—the things that belong to him, and give to God the things that belong to Him.)
- Ephesians 5:15-17 (Make good use of every opportunity.)

Write each verse and a summary of each group's findings on the board.

5 Three Case Studies

Describe each of the following situations, one at a time. Ask volunteers to offer suggestions about what they might say (or do) to help the individual in each case. Challenge group members to apply the passages studied previously to these situations.

- *Case 1*—George. He used to be the most active member of this group. He was there every time the doors opened. Then he got involved in the school drama club. He became a member of the yearbook staff and started dating a girl in the

French club. He joined a Tai-Kwan-Do class, and spends two nights a week punching the stuffing out of mattresses. He says he just never has time for the activities of this group. You miss George. He was a lot of fun to be around.

• *Case 2*—Tom. He's never been to your church. That's too bad because you think he's a pretty nice guy and that he'd offer a lot to your group. Sheree, one of your best friends, agrees with you and suggests that you both invite him to attend an upcoming event. You corner Tom in the hall and offer the invitation. He just smiles, says, "Thanks, but I'm just too busy," and walks away. Later your mother tells you she met Tom's mom at a PTA meeting, and she said he never does anything with anyone. He just sits in his room, alone, each night.

• *Case 3*—Joyce. Of course you like Joyce, one of your youth group sponsors. Who wouldn't? She gives every waking minute of her life to your youth group. If she's not at the church planning a program or retreat, she's on the phone with one kid while making a batch of brownies for another. You guys are always at Joyce's house, and she and her husband John have always welcomed you openly—until lately. It seems like John is getting a little tired of the group. Maybe that's because Joyce always has time for the group, but she has no time for her family.

6 Setting Goals

Say something like: **If we agree that the argument, "I really don't have time for the youth group," is really a statement of priorities, perhaps we should look at how to better structure our time. Hundreds of magazine articles have been published about time management. Actually, most just offer five or ten practical steps for managing time. In fact, they're so practical, I'll bet that we could come up with ten sensible steps right now.**

Brainstorm together and list as many practical things that one can do to manage time. (Your group might suggest things like: "Take time to smell the roses"; "Learn to say no"; "Delegate jobs to other people"; "Figure out how to do several things at the same time"; "Give up something," etc.)

Pass out copies of Student Sheet 8-B ("Goal Mining") to group members. Encourage them to create their own lists of personal goals (have daily devotions; get a part-time job; improve my grade in a subject, etc.) by working through the steps of the worksheet. After everyone has completed his or her worksheet, ask each group member to find a partner to witness his or her plan by signing the bottom of the worksheet. Challenge partners to help support one another in their efforts to accomplish their goals.

Close this session in prayer, thanking God for the time He's given, and for the challenges that we have to accomplish within our time limits. Also, ask for help in providing support for each other's personal goals.

Clock Work

Examine each of the following types of clocks. Write the name of each member of your group beneath the clock that reminds you most of him or her.

Grandfather Clock

The "wise one" of the group. It's been around awhile, and has the scrapes, scratches, and scars to prove it. Of course, it misses a beat or two every now and then, but basically, it's reliable.

Alarm Clock

This clock lets people know when something alarming is about to happen. It warns of deadlines or potential dangers, and generally wakes people up. The problem is, when it goes off, you're not always ready for it.

Stopwatch

Used for testing. Always trying to make sure the group is doing its very best. Keeps the group on the task at hand.

Timex

"Takes a licking and keeps on ticking." Always back for more, no matter what happens to it. Very trustworthy.

Electronic Watch

The brains of the outfit, it's got all kinds of computerized gadgetry. Smart? You bet. If you've got a question, this one's usually got the answer.

Rolex

Let's face it—this is classy. It's valuable. It's seen as important by many. It's desirable. And it's built to withstand the test of time.

Clock Tower

Stands like a beacon for everyone in the community to see. It's majestic and proud. People look for it to find out where they should go and when they should get there.

Dick Tracy Watch Radio

This handy little item is great for communicating. It passes the word on to whoever needs to know whenever he or she needs to know.

Clock Radio

Wanna keep a beat while you keep on time? This is just the thing. Up on fashion, trends, and popular events. Very timely.

GOAL MINING

What are your short-term goals? What do you want to accomplish in the near future? Use this worksheet to come up with a working plan.

SURVEYING THE LAND

What do you want to accomplish? On the lines below list ten things that you'd like to do in the next six months.

______________________ ______________________
______________________ ______________________
______________________ ______________________
______________________ ______________________
______________________ ______________________

STAKING A CLAIM

Narrow your list to four items. Write them next to the "Goal" headings. Be as specific as you can.

Goal ______________________ Deadline __________

Steps ______________________
____
____

Goal ______________________ Deadline __________

Steps ______________________
____
____

Goal ______________________ Deadline __________

Steps ______________________
____
____

Goal ______________________ Deadline __________

Steps ______________________
____
____

Working the Mine

Write a specific date for accomplishing your goal next to the "Deadline" heading (write "weekly" for on-going goals), and three specific things that you'll need to do to reach that goal in the "Steps" column.

[Example: To accomplish the goal of raising his grade to a "B" in history, Brian set a deadline of March 23, and decided to meet weekly in a study group with other students, to rewrite his notes every night, and to read 30 pages of history every week.]

Signing the Deed

Finally, to seal the deal, ask a friend to sign his or her name below, promising to support you in your efforts to reach your four goals.

Witnessed by: ______________________________________

Session 9

When it comes to reading the Bible, most kids wish there were Cliff Notes. The same goes for practicing the Christian lifestyle; it seems like it's just too hard. But most things worth anything in life take a bit of effort, and Christianity is certainly no exception. In fact, after kids expend the effort necessary to understand the Bible or a Christian principle, they are usually more committed to it.

It's important to help kids recognize that there *are* tough things about living the Christian life. If we promise easy answers, our kids will stumble when the going gets unexpectedly rough. This session can reveal your group members' struggles with a life of faith and then help them discover ways to overcome those hurdles.

"Christianity/The Bible Is Too Hard"

Specific Aim

• To help kids understand that most things of value require hard work to attain; to help them give voice to what they believe is hard about the Bible/Christianity; and to give them an opportunity to brainstorm solutions to the obstacles that confront them.

Scriptural Support

- Psalm 1:1-3
- Philippians 2:12, 13
- II Timothy 2:15; 3:16, 17
- Hebrews 12:1, 2

Special Preparation

- Bibles
- Copies of Student Sheet 9-A ("I Did It!")
- One copy of Student Sheet 9-B ("A Stone and a Snake")
- Pencils
- Prizes for "Two Truths and a Lie"
- Paper
- Envelopes

1 Two Truths and a Lie

Divide into three small groups and pass out paper and pencils. In the groups, each person should tell the others three things he or she has accomplished that took some hard work (i.e., getting on the basketball squad, earning straight "A" grades one semester, climbing the stairs to the top of the Washington Monument). Two of these accomplishments should be real, but one should be invented. Other group members should try to guess which statement is the lie and write that statement on their papers. After each has had a turn, everyone should reveal his or her lie. Award points for correct guesses. Give a prize to the best guesser in each group.

2 I Did It!

Say something like: **We've all done things that took extra effort. Here's your chance to document some of those achievements for posterity.** Hand out Student Sheet 9-A ("I Did It!"), which asks group members to list their most important achievements. After they have completed their lists, you may want to ask them to share the top five items with the members of their small groups.

Say: **Look at those items which are most important to you. Generally speaking, are your most important accomplishments those that took the most effort?** (Probably, though you may have some kids who will argue this point with you.)

Why do important things take more effort? (Perhaps the effort is what makes them important. We are willing to work harder at the things we think are worth the work.)

Does it necessarily follow that the things that require the most work are also the most important to us? (You may receive different opinions here. The important thing to acknowledge is that we do value things we have to work for.)

3 For the Sake of Argument

Ask: **In your opinion, is it difficult to be a Christian today? Why or why not? Do you think it's harder to live a Christian life today than it was 50 years ago? 100 years ago?**

Is studying the Bible tough in today's world?

After a few minutes of spontaneous debate, divide the group into two teams. One team should list as many arguments as it can that point out it's easier to live a Christian life today than it was 50 or 100 years ago. (We live in a society that supports freedom of religion, allowing us to choose our beliefs. We have so many more resources than Christians have ever had before. We can read; until 75 years ago, many people were illiterate).

The other team should come up with as many arguments as it can supporting the premise that it's more difficult to be a Christian today. (There are so many more temptations and distractions than ever before. Because of international communication, we face more choices concerning faith, entertainment, lifestyle, etc.) After a few minutes of brainstorming, let each group share its findings.

Sum up the groups' findings by saying something like: **As you can see, in some ways, it's harder to be a Christian today than in the past. In other ways, it's easier.**

4 Why Try?

Ask: **Why should we work so hard to live lives that are pleasing to God?** Explain that you are going to read several reasons for trying to please God, and you want group members to vote on each. If they believe it's a good reason, they should stand up. If they think it's a poor reason, they should cross their arms over their chests.

- **We should work hard to please God because the Bible says to.**
- **We should work hard to please God because we want to go to heaven.** (You may want to point out that this attitude misses the point of God's free gift of salvation.)
- **We should work hard to please God so we won't go to hell.**
- **We should work hard to please God because our best friends do.**
- **We should work hard to please God because our parents want us to.**
- **We should work hard to please God because we'll be better people.**
- **We should work hard to please God because the world needs a good example.**
- **We should work hard to please God because we'll be glad we did when we get older.**
- **We should work hard to please God so we won't feel guilty.**

Have volunteers read aloud the following Scripture passages. Ask group members to summarize the biblical reasons for living the Christian life and studying the Bible.

- Psalm 1:1-3 (Understanding God's laws and living by them can help us to have a firm foundation—like a deeply rooted tree—and prosper accordingly.)
- Philippians 2:12, 13 (God will work in our lives as we obey Him.)
- II Timothy 2:15; 3:16, 17 (God's Word can teach us and keep us on the right path, so we need to be able to understand and depend on it.)

5 A Stone and a Snake

Say something like: **You know, there might just be a valid reason why Christianity and studying the Bible are so difficult. Sometimes hard work can make something a little more important to us. Here's a parable that illustrates what I**

mean. Ask a volunteer to read the story from Student Sheet 9-B ("A Stone and a Snake").

Afterward, ask group members how the story made them feel and what thoughts came to mind during the reading.

Ask: **How did the man in the parable help his son?** (He taught the boy to fulfill his own needs through fishing and making bread).

Wouldn't it have been easier to give the boy what he asked for? (The son would not have learned independence, and would not have grown without the challenge of doing things himself.)

What might you learn from having to figure out a tough Bible verse?

How could it strengthen your faith by having to believe in God without seeing Him?

How could having to say no to temptation actually help you?

6 Running the Great Race

Ask a volunteer to read Hebrews 12:1, 2 aloud. Say: **In a sense, the Christian life is like a race. It takes work, and discipline, and a lot of effort. Where would you say you are, right now, in the race that Paul writes about?**

Divide everyone into the small groups from Step 1. Ask group members to think about where they are in their Christian race:

- Are they at the starting line, ready to begin?
- Are they rounding the first or second turn, and picking up speed?
- Are they on the sidelines, waiting to get in the race?
- Are they on the cheerleading squad, encouraging others to do their best?
- Are they in the grandstands, watching all of the action?
- Are they visiting the snack bar, totally oblivious to the race?
- Are they in the locker room, having tossed in the towel?

Now, ask group members to share with their small groups where they would like to be in this great race of faith.

Allow a few minutes for each small group to talk about what makes studying the Bible or living the Christian life so difficult. (Making time to do it; understanding concepts and words; knowing where to start, etc.)

Encourage people to share suggestions or ideas that have worked for them in overcoming the obstacles listed by each group.

Pass out paper, pencils, and envelopes to group members. Ask them to think about where they would like to be in their spiritual race three months from now. What would they like to have accomplished by that time? Ask each person to write a letter to himself or herself expressing his or her hopes. When they are all finished, ask them to place the letters in the envelopes, seal them, and write their mailing addresses on the envelopes. Collect these letters and explain that you will mail them in three months, so group members can be reminded of their hopes and plans.

Close in prayer, asking God to help everyone have the discipline and desire to work to grow in his or her faith.

I Did It!

We've all done things we are very proud of. Some kids are members of athletic teams. Some excel by playing a musical instrument. Others make great grades. Some kids work at being the greatest friends in the world. What are you proud of that you've done?

List several of your accomplishments in the column on the left. (These may include things like never forgetting to take out the garbage, winning a pie-eating contest, figuring out how to use a computer, etc.) On the right, jot down a note to indicate how much effort each item took (time, energy, competition, etc.). Then place a star beside the five accomplishments that you consider to be most important.

Oh, by the way—congratulations!

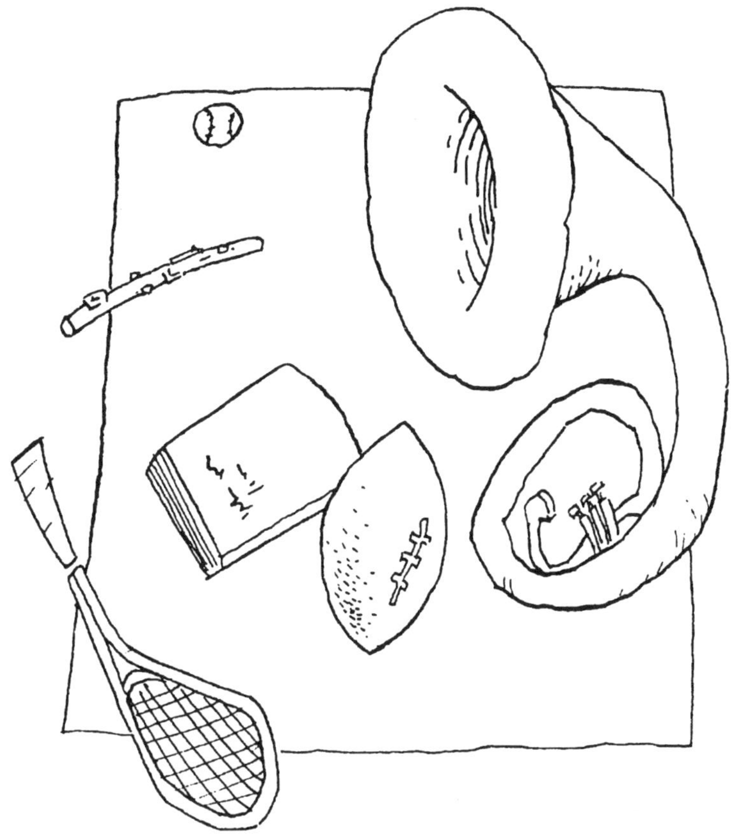

WHAT I DID	***WHAT IT TOOK***
______________________________	__________________
______________________________	__________________
______________________________	__________________
______________________________	__________________
______________________________	__________________
______________________________	__________________
______________________________	__________________
______________________________	__________________
______________________________	__________________
______________________________	__________________

A Stone and a Snake

Once there was a successful man. He lived in a small town and was recognized by all as a wise and hard-working person. He was standing in the courtyard one day with several other influential people when his young son approached. The boy tugged on his father's cloak.

"Father, Father," he cried insistently.

The man knelt down beside his son. "Yes?"

"Father, can I have a sweet roll?" the son asked, pointing to the bakery on the other side of the courtyard.

The father looked across the street at the bakery. He owned the bakery and paid the baker fine wages to create the tasty sweet rolls. Slowly he turned back to face his son.

"No," he said.

Then, taking a large, smooth stone from the pocket of his garment, he gave it to his son and said, "But if you'll take this stone into the shop and tell the baker who you are, he'll let you use it to grind grain on his pestle and he'll help you bake your own sweet roll."

The son looked puzzled. Hadn't he just asked for a sweet roll? He didn't want a stone; he wanted something to eat. Turning his gaze, he spied the fishery down by the lake. It had large nets draped over the doorway and window. A soft sea breeze floated up from the water.

"Fish!" the boy exclaimed. "Let's get some fish."

The father paused for a moment while his young son screamed impatiently for some fish. Then he turned and walked to a nearby flower bed. As his son watched, he dug up a bit of earth with his hand. Turning the soil over and over he unearthed a long, dark, slithering creature. He clenched it firmly in his hands, as it tried to crawl away. He handed the creature to his son.

The little boy stared a question into the wise man's face.

"Take the earthworm, use the hook and line from our house, and you can catch your own fish," the father explained.

That afternoon, the boy caught and cleaned his first fish. While it was cooking over the fire, he ground wheat in the baker's pestle and baked a small loaf of bread. He shared his meal with his father and mother that night.

When he grew up, the little boy owned a bakery and a fishery. And he was considered to be very wise and very successful indeed.

Session 10

"Sometimes, being cool is not so hot."—Ward Cleaver (All-American dad, *Leave It to Beaver)*

Even though Mr. Cleaver tried to dispel the desire to be cool among children in the 1950s, kids today still want to be cool. After all, cool means never having to say you're sorry. Cool means never being alone, or rejected, or ugly.

But the church is the one place where a young person should never worry about being alone, or rejected, or ugly. The church, when it really lives up to its high calling, is better than cool.

"It's Not Cool to Get Involved in the Church"

Specific Aim

• To help kids recognize that going to church can be as "cool" as they want to make it; and to help them brainstorm reasons why going to church seems "uncool" and potential answers for each objection.

Scriptural Support

• Matthew 20:20-28; 23:8-12
• Mark 9:33-37
• Romans 12:1-3
• Philippians 2:1-11

Special Preparation

• Bibles
• Cut-apart cards from Student Sheet 10-A ("Cool Cards")
• Copies of Student Sheet 10-B ("Time for a Cool Change")
• Pencils
• Chalkboard and chalk or newsprint and marker

1 One Thing I Like

Ask everyone to sit in a large circle. Go around the circle and ask each person to complete the following sentence: "One thing I like about the people in this group is . . . "

Give everyone a chance to share, but also the opportunity to pass. After everyone has completed the sentence, say something like: **The members of this group have a lot going for them. Would you say that the members of this group are cool?** (You'll probably receive different responses. Some might say that it depends on what you mean by "cool.") **Would you say that participating in the group is cool?** (Again, different responses. Some people may think that being in the group is cool.) **Would popular people in your school agree with you?** (Probably not.)

2 A Cool Definition

Divide the group into four teams. Give each team one of the following assignments:

Team A: Come up with your best definition of "cool."

Team B: Name five truly cool people living in our world today.

Team C: List five things that cool people do.

Team D: List five things that cool people don't do.

Ask: **Bottom line, what is it that makes someone cool?** (They may say something like, "A cool person is someone that everyone else likes or envies.")

Say something like: **So, supposing you could be cool, what would it get you?** (Acceptance, friends, popularity, etc.)

Say: **Let's create an imaginary person. We'll name him "Chris." Now Chris is one of the coolest people in the school. Someone describe "Chris" for me.** Give several people a chance to share their image of how Chris would look, act, talk, etc. Ask everyone to remember this image of Chris for a later activity.

3 A Cool Game

Place the "Cool Cards" from Student Sheet 10-A on a table in the middle of the room. Put some chairs on the right side of the room and some on the left. Invite everyone to line up single file in the middle of the room. Explain that you're going to play a little game. Everyone will draw a card, read it, and follow its instructions. Point out the sets of chairs on the right and left sides of the room. Explain that the chairs on the right side are for "cool" people. Those on the left side are for "others."

Begin the game. Let each person draw a card, read it aloud, and go to the side of the room that the card indicates. If there are no empty chairs left, he or she should sit on the lap of someone else sitting on that side of the room. As crowds start to gather on either side of the room, encourage wild cheering, catcalls, etc. Give volunteers a chance to draw a second card, if there are cards left over after everyone has taken his or her turn. (This activity depends totally on the "luck of the draw," so no one will really be put down.)

After everyone has had a chance to draw a card, ask: **How does it feel to be in the cool seats right now?** (Special; better than the others; elite, etc.)

How does it feel not to be in the cool seats right now? (Left out; envious; uncomfortable, etc.)

Do the cards accurately describe what is and what isn't cool?

To the "uncool" group, say: **We know that none of the things on our cool cards really happened, but isn't it natural to feel a little left out or defensive because you're in a group that's labeled "uncool?"**

So, is it cool to be a Christian? Would "Chris" be a Christian?

4 Tough Cases

Divide into the four small groups you used earlier. Give each group one of the following Scripture passages and the situation accompanying it. Ask group members to read the passage and decide what response Jesus would recommend for their situation.

Team A—Matthew 20:20-28

Situation: You and your friends have just come from a super-charged pep rally. You're fired up and so are the athletes on your team. Just then a kid with a Bible under his arm confronts your group. "Don't you know," he says, "that no one should claim they are the greatest! You shouldn't be so proud and boastful. Pride is a sin. Read Matthew 20:20-28."

Team B—Matthew 23:8-12

Situation: Your parents have been quite successful lately. They've worked hard and managed to earn a bit of money. Your family moved into a larger house, and everyone in town seems proud of you. Your little brother has started saying that the neighbors from your old subdivision (in a poorer neighborhood) are second-rate.

Team C—Mark 9:33-37

Situation: Some of your friends are bad-mouthing Jewish people. They say that Jewish people are cheap and lazy. One guy's got a magazine that presents information in a manner that is demeaning to Jews. What do you do?

Team D—Philippians 2:1-11

Situation: Everyone's going out for pizza after the game on Friday night. However, your school service club had planned an all-nighter at the local homeless shelter, helping homeless people. You know you could get out of the project if you wanted to. Do you try?

Give each group a chance to share its Scripture passage and situations with the other groups. Ask: **How do you think "Chris" would act in these situations?** (Some might say that Chris would be selfish and cruel. Others might say Chris could be as committed to Christ as anyone else and respond appropriately.)

How do you think Christ would act in these situations?

Ask someone to read Romans 12:1-3 aloud. Ask: **What does Paul tell you in this passage about being "cool?"** You might say that a cool person is one who serves as a living sacrifice, giving himself or herself over to God's will. The important thing is not living by the world's definition of cool, but by God's.

5 Chris's Crossroads

Say: **What would you think if I said that Chris once told me, "It's not cool to get involved in church?"** (Some might say it's his loss. Others might say that he doesn't know what he's talking about.)

Divide into two groups. Ask the first group to list as many things as it can that are cool about the youth group. Ask the other group to come up with as many things as it can that a "cool" person might not care for. Ask each group to write its lists on the board. After a few minutes, ask one person from each group to share his or her list with the entire group.

I believe that guys like Chris need the church. And they don't have to be "uncool" to be involved. What are some specific things we can change to better reach out to those who think that getting involved in the church is not cool? Write these suggestions on the board.

Pass out copies of Student Sheet 10-B ("Time for a Cool Change"). Give everyone time to fill out the survey. You might choose to pass these along to your youth leadership group as an evaluation tool in planning.

6 Closing Circle

Have everyone form a circle. Ask someone to read Romans 12:1-3 again. Then go around the circle and have each person share one thing that he or she has learned during this session. It can be serious or funny, but each person should try to come up with one thing. If someone wants to pass, however, let him or her. You should begin the sharing process.

Close in prayer, thanking God for everyone who is attending the group. Thank Him for the fun your group members have together, and for their own unique brand of "cool." Ask for guidance on how to reach out to those who have misconceptions about the church and for strength to follow through.

Cool Cards

You just became the school photographer and have won fame and acceptance all over the campus (when you have your camera with you). Go to the right side.

Your father is a minister. Explain in your own words how this can be cool or not cool. Go to the side of the room that you choose to explain.

One of the best-looking people in the world just asked you out on a date! Go to the right side.

You make great grades. In fact, several people have asked you to be in their study groups. Go to the right side.

Someone extra special turned you down for a date—in front of most of the people in your class. Go to the left side.

Class bullies have chosen you as their "shrimp of the year." Go to the left side.

Your ancient, dilapidated car stalls in the middle of the street right after school lets out. Go to the left side.

Your blow-dryer blew a fuse—for the fifth time this week. Go to the left side.

You've just been given the nickname, "Turkey." Go to the left side.

You've made the football, baseball, and basketball teams. Way to go! Take a seat on the bench—on the right side.

You burped during lunch. Go to the left side.

You were sitting in the school cafeteria when the Youth Director walked in. He asked you to introduce him to all of your friends. Go to the left side.

You go to school with your clothes wrinkled. Go to the left side.

You failed to make the football, baseball, basketball, or cheerleading squads. Sorry! Go to the left side.

Your father is one of the most popular businessmen in your town. He's successful and people look to you for the same kind of success. Go to the right side.

Your dad just won $10,000,000 from Ed McMahon. Everyone's talking about it. Go to the right side.

Time for a Cool Change

What do you think is cool about youth group and church activities? How can they be improved? Complete the following survey and give it to your leader.

Put a check mark in the "Cool" column if you think the activity is OK as is. Put a check mark in the "Not-So-Hot" column if you think the activity needs work. Then offer a suggestion or two for how the activity could be improved.

Youth Group Activities	***Cool***	***Not-So-Hot***	***Suggestions***
Bible studies			
Group singing			
Group recreation			
Parties			
Group trips			
Group retreats			
Service projects			
Mission trips			
Other ______________			
Other ______________			
Church Activities	***Cool***	***Not-So-Hot***	***Suggestions***
Worship services			
Hymns			
Choir anthems			
Children's sermon			
Prayers			
Other ______________			
Other ______________			

Session 11

We've all got them in our youth groups—kids who just don't want to do the work. One study of younger teens indicated that 47.7% of kids who are church members never attend their youth program. Only about 31% of the kids in this study said they'd be interested in participating in a church-sponsored program aimed at doing "something good for other people." The unfortunate thing about kids who want to let somebody else do the work is that they're missing out on the *process* of being a Christian. They can't grow spiritually because they never practice their faith.

Some kids are uninvolved because they think they have nothing to offer. It's important to assure these kids that they have *much* to offer. They may not be modern-day Pauls or Peters, but they might identify with basketball player Stacey King. At the end of an NBA game, King was quoted as saying, "I'll always remember this as the night that Michael Jordan and I combined to score 70 points." Jordan scored 69 points that night. Yet Stacey King still had something to offer. Chicago had won the game by one point. Maybe King wasn't a superstar like Michael Jordan, but he made a critical contribution. Encourage your kids to do the same.

"Let Somebody Else Do the Work"

Specific Aim

- To help kids understand that God's commands—and His rewards—are not just directed to the "spiritual giants" of the faith, but to everyone; and to affirm the potential of every kid to be a difference-maker in the world.

Scriptural Support

- Jeremiah 1:4-10
- Matthew 9:9-13; 19:16-24
- Mark 1:14-18
- Acts 9:3-9, 17-19
- Galatians 5:22, 23
- Ephesians 4:3-7, 11-16

Special Preparation

- Bibles
- Copies of Student Sheet 11-A ("Call and Response")
- Copies of Student Sheet 11-B ("A Bowl of Fruit")
- Pencils
- Chalkboard and chalk or newsprint and marker
- Classified advertisement section of local newspaper
- Paper

1 Tell Us about Yourself

Pass out pencils and paper. Ask each group member to write ten words that describe himself or herself. Instruct group members not to put their names on the papers. When everyone is finished, explain that you'll be using these sheets later in the session.

Bring everyone together in one large circle. Go around the circle and have each person share about a time when he or she felt important (participating in a sport, performing in the school play, completing a big assignment or job responsibility, etc.). You should set the tone by beginning, then give everyone in the circle a chance to share. (If your group is large, break into smaller groups for this activity.)

2 Help Wanted

Bring in the classified advertising section of your local newspaper. Read a few "Help Wanted" advertisements. Have your kids form small groups. Ask group members to imagine that God wants them to find people who will help carry out His plan for the world. Give each group paper and pencils, and have each group write its own classified ad to find these people. After a few minutes, ask each group to share its ad with the rest of the groups. (You might want to place some of these ads in your church or youth group newsletter.)

Ask: **What kinds of people do you think God wants to do His work? What specific skills, experiences, or abilities do you think they should possess?**

Have each person place his or her self-description sheet in the center of the circle. Ask volunteers to shuffle the papers and then look through them to see if any of the "résumés" fit their want ads. Do they describe people that God would want to do His work, according to their classified advertisements? Collect the information for a later activity.

3 Answering the Call

Distribute copies of Student Sheet 11-A ("Call and Response"). Divide your group into five small groups. Assign each small group one of the passages of Scripture, and ask each group to complete its part of the chart. (If your group is small, divide into fewer groups and assign more than one passage to each group.) After everyone has finished, ask a volunteer from each group to describe the passage and share how his or her group completed the chart.

Use the following suggested answers to supplement your discussion:

Jeremiah 1:4-10—Jeremiah; unborn child; challenge to be prophet; made excuses; promised His help.

Matthew 9:9-13—Matthew; tax collector; nothing; followed; accepted Matthew and his friends.

Matthew 19:16-24—Ruler; rich and young; eternal life; went away sad; said it was hard for rich people to enter heaven.

Mark 1:14-18—Simon and Andrew; fishermen; to make them fishers of men; dropped nets and followed; continued to teach them.

Acts 9:3-9, 17-19—Saul; religious leader; relationship and the Holy Spirit; obeyed; restored his sight.

Say something like: **Think about these six people. They were all so different. Some were famous leaders. Some were common people. Which do you relate to the most? Notice that Jesus empowered those who chose to follow Him, regardless of who they were or what they had done before they met Him. Don't you think that He could do the same with your life?**

4 Meet Donna

Introduce a fictitious character to focus the attention on the issue at hand. Say something like: **Let me introduce you to Donna. She's a great kid. She has a lot going for her; people enjoy her company, and she's bright and cheerful. She's talented. She makes enviable grades. There's one thing, however, about Donna. Whenever possible, she sits back and lets everyone else do all the work. Donna's not on any leadership teams in school or church. She doesn't help plan events or programs. Donna participates when she has the time, but doesn't worry if she misses several activities—particularly the outreach activities.**

During this session, try to think about how to apply what we're talking about to Donna. What could she learn that might help her? What could you say to Donna that might encourage her?

Oh, by the way, Donna doesn't really exist. But thinking about her will help us understand the people like her who *are* real.

What excuses do you think Donna would make about not getting involved in the activities of this group? (She doesn't have time; she'll let others do the work; she has more important things to do, etc.)

How do you think Donna would have reacted if Jesus had approached her as He did some of the people listed on our chart? (Chances are that she might have turned Him down as the rich young ruler did).

5 Experiencing the Body of Christ

Ask a volunteer to read Ephesians 4:3-7, 11-16. Divide back into the five groups used earlier. Play a quick game of "People Machines." Assign each group one of the following machines. The task is to create the "machine" using only the members of the group (and any sound effects they can create). The other groups will attempt to guess what they are acting out.

Suggested machines include a roller coaster, a video camera, an automobile, a vending machine, and a fax machine.

After each group has had a chance to act out its machine, ask the volunteer to read again the passage from Ephesians. Ask: **What comparison is there between this passage and the machines we've created?** (Just as every person had a task in creating the machines, so every person has a task as a Christian.)

Ask one of the groups to enact its machine again, except this time pull a key member out of the group. Ask: **How did the machine work without that one person?** (It probably didn't work as well.) **What do you think the message is for our fictitious friend Donna?** (We all have parts to play in being members of the Body of Christ.)

6 Filling the Fruit Bowl

Pass out copies of Student Sheet 11-B ("A Bowl of Fruit"). Ask each person to read Galatians 5:22, 23 (at the top of the sheet) and to fill in the names of the different people in his or her small group in the blank spaces beside each fruit of the Spirit. Encourage group members to indicate why they think each person demonstrates that fruit in his or her life.

After everyone has finished, ask each person to share his or her choices with the rest of the small group. Group members should tell which fruit of the Spirit they assigned to each person in their groups and explain how that person demonstrates that fruit.

After each person has shared from his or her worksheet, go around the circle again and ask each person to identify the fruit of the Spirit he or she would like to demonstrate more of in his or her life.

Ask: **How does knowing that others think you possess certain abilities make you feel?** (Proud, humble, warm inside, a little scared, etc.)

If the person sitting on your right decided not to get involved, do you think it would affect our group? (Sure. We'd miss the good things that person adds to our group.)

Based on this passage, if you were to talk to our friend "Donna," what might you say to encourage her to share her part of the workload? (You could say she has certain abilities the group would miss when she didn't participate. If she were patient, for instance, you might say that patience adds a calming effect to the group, and the group would be more obnoxious without her.)

7 Closing Prayer

Randomly take three or four of the self-description sheets from the stack used earlier. Explain that you are going to close in a group prayer. You will pray, and each time you pause, group members should pray in unison, "We thank You for placing this person in our lives."

Use the following pattern for your closing prayer:

Thank You, Father for the work of Your Spirit in this group. Thank You for people like "Donna," who really do have a lot to offer our group. Please encourage people like Donna to allow themselves to get involved, so they can grow through the experience.

I especially thank You for the involvement of a person who is . . . (Read the items from one of the sheets.)

GROUP: We thank You for placing this person in our lives.

I thank You for another person who participates in our group. This person is . . . (Read the items from one of the sheets.)

GROUP: We thank You for placing this person in our lives.

Thank You for this individual. He is . . . (Read the items from one of the sheets.)

GROUP: We thank You for placing this person in our lives.

(If time permits, you may want to add a few more sheets.)

For all of these people that You allow to share our lives, we thank You, Lord. Amen.

CALL AND RESPONSE

Passage	Who was called?	Describe the person(s)	What was offered?	What did the person do?	The Lord's response?
Jeremiah 1:4-10					
Matthew 9:9-13					
Matthew 19:16-24					
Mark 1:14-18					
Acts 9:3-9, 17-19					

A Bowl of Fruit

"But the fruit of the Spirit is love, joy, peace, patience, kindness, goodness, faithfulness, gentleness, and self-control" (Galatians 5:22, 23).

Think of the people in your small group. Which kinds of fruit of the Spirit have you seen in their lives? Which individuals seem to demonstrate love in all they do? Which are joyful people? Is one of your group members a peaceful individual?

Write everyone's names in the blank spaces on the left. Draw a line to the quality on the right that you have seen the person demonstrate. Then, write why you chose that fruit for that person.

Name	*Fruit of the Spirit*
______________________ Why?	Love
______________________ Why?	Joy
______________________ Why?	Peace
______________________ Why?	Patience
______________________ Why?	Kindness
______________________ Why?	Goodness
______________________ Why?	Faithfulness
______________________ Why?	Gentleness
______________________ Why?	Self-control

Session 12

When your kids say, "This group is too small," don't take it personally. It's too easy to blame ourselves if our youth groups aren't the biggest in the state. After all—the argument goes—if we were good leaders, the kids would attend. Well, that's usually not the case. Church demographics, rather than leadership, often determine the number of teenagers likely to attend.

Remember, *bigger* isn't necessarily *better.* Sometimes a small group can be more spiritually alive than a large group. After all, it's impossible for kids to stay "invisible" in a small group. Instead of a *complaint,* the statement, "This group is too small," just might be a *request*—for more friends or more variety. It may also be a starting point to challenge kids in your group to invite their friends. And when they're motivated to bring their friends, they usually stop worrying about the group's size.

"The Group Is Too Small"

Specific Aim

• To help kids recognize the opportunity for close fellowship in a small group; to help them understand that it's not the size of a group that matters—it's the commitment; and to help kids brainstorm ways to help the group grow.

Scriptural Support

• Matthew 13:31, 32; 18:10-14, 20
• Mark 6:7-12
• Luke 10:1-12
• Acts 2:40-47; 6:1-7; 9:31

Special Preparation

• Bibles
• Copies of Student Sheet 12-A ("What's the Best Body Size?")
• Copies of Student Sheet 12-B ("Who You Gonna Call?")
• Pencils
• Chalkboard and chalk or newsprint and marker
• Before the meeting you might ask one or two of your young people to "scope out the competition" by attending a local youth group that is larger than yours. Ask them to bring back suggestions and perceptions to discuss in your group.

1 Are You More Like . . . ?

Place the chairs in several rows and ask each person to take a seat. Explain that each row symbolizes a single line—a continuum. You are going to read several questions that ask, "Are you more like . . . ?" Group members should move to the left of their rows if they are like the first part of the question and to the right if they are more like the second part of the question. If they are not like either, they should find a seat in the middle of their rows.

For example, you might ask, "Are you more like an opera or a rock concert?" Everyone who enjoys an opera the most would move to one of the seats on the left of the row. Everyone who likes rock music would move to one of the seats on the right of the row. Those who liked both would stay seated in the middle of the row.

(NOTE: If someone is already sitting on a chair that best represents an individual's preference, that individual should sit on the person's lap.)

You may want to supplement the following questions with your own versions that incorporate special references to your church or area:

- **Are you more like New York City or** (mention a nearby small town)?
- **Are you more like a 747 airliner or a Piper Cub?**
- **Are you more like a barbecue dinner or a seven-course gourmet meal?**
- **Are you more like rap music or rock and roll?**
- **Are you more like a small, cozy gathering or a large, rowdy party?**
- **Are you more like a deep blue ocean or a rushing stream?**
- **Are you more like a rainy night or a sunny day?**
- **Are you more like pizza or steak?**
- **Are you more like the live theater or a video movie?**

Ask: **What observations can you make from this exercise about our group? If you were to describe the members of this group to someone who didn't know any of them, what would you say?** In discussion, be sure to point out what a unique group you have, full of special individuals who all add to the group's distinctive character.

2 "I Wish" Votes

Introduce this voting exercise by explaining that you are going to name several things that kids might want. When you name an item group members want, they should raise their hands.

- **I wish I had a jam-packed agenda with fun things to do every weekend.**
- **I wish I had straight A's.**
- **I wish I were taller.**
- **I wish I were shorter.**
- **I wish I knew someone who could tell me exactly what to say in tough situations.**
- **I wish I had a thorough understanding of the Bible.**

- **I wish I had a wonderful singing voice.**
- **I wish I had a few close friends to talk to when I'm down.**
- **I wish this youth group had more guys in it.**
- **I wish this youth group had more girls in it.**
- **I wish this youth group were larger.**

Say something like: **There are a number of different ingredients for youth groups. Right now we want to focus on the statement, "I wish this youth group were larger."**

Ask if any of your group members have ever attended larger youth groups. If so, ask them to tell you what the experience was like.

Ask: **What was good about the bigger group?** (More variety, enthusiasm, excitement.)

What wasn't so good? (It's easy to get lost in a big group.)

3 Scripture Search

Explain to your group members that you're going to be taking a look at Scripture to discover strengths of both larger and smaller groups. Divide your group into four teams. Cut Student Sheet 12-A ("What's the Best Body Size?") into four pieces, and give each team one of the pieces. Ask each team to read the two passages of Scripture on its card and decide how those biblical principles can be applied to worshiping and serving God in small or large groups.

Scripture doesn't say whether larger or smaller groups are ideal for worship. The early church was represented by two or three believers at times and, at other times, it included thousands. There are passages on each card to support the need for both large and small groups. Possible summaries are as follows:

- Matthew 13:31, 32 (Small things—such as small groups—have the potential to make big changes.)
- Matthew 18:10-14 (What may seem insignificant to us may be very important to the Lord.)
- Matthew 18:20 (Even two or three people can experience Christ's presence in their midst.)
- Mark 6:7-12 (Teams of two were able to do powerful work for the Lord.)
- Luke 10:1-12 (The Lord empowered some very small groups—pairs of disciples—to carry out His mission. But He charged a large number of people—70—to reach the various areas.)
- Acts 2:40-47 (There is strength in numbers and an increased ability to share resources.)
- Acts 6:1-7 (A large group can divide up the work, sharing responsibility to care for group members.)
- Acts 9:31 (When the Lord is at work, people want to become part of it.)

After each team has studied its passage, ask group members to report their findings to everyone.

Say: **From these passages of Scripture, the Bible seems to indicate that there are times when large groups are most effective, and times when smaller groups**

are better. Basically, the Bible doesn't seem to place a value judgment on size.

Have two of the groups brainstorm together to think of advantages that smaller groups have over larger groups. (Smaller groups are often more intimate; smaller groups usually don't have problems with cliques; smaller groups are easier to keep from getting out of control, etc.)

Ask the other two groups to brainstorm together and come up with advantages that larger groups have over smaller groups. (Larger groups usually offer a bigger variety of things to do and people to know; larger groups generate momentum and excitement; you can get tired of the people in smaller groups.)

Give each group a chance to share its findings with the entire group.

4 Experiencing Differences in Size

Tell the group that you want to participate in an exercise to help them experience the emotions of being in larger or smaller groups. Clear things away from the center of the room and ask everyone to find a spot on the floor. Turn the lights down low. Ask everyone to close his or her eyes and listen carefully to your voice.

Think for a moment about your favorite place to go when you want to be by yourself. Perhaps it's your bedroom, or a place outdoors, or a sanctuary. Picture that place in your mind and think about being there. At times it's good to be alone. It gives us time to reflect on important things. It gives us a chance to catch our breath.

Continue after a few minutes: **Now think of a time when you were in a large crowd. Maybe a football game or shopping in a crowded mall. Picture yourself being jostled by the crowd around you. Think about trying to go in one direction when the crowd is heading the other way. It's tough when you're caught up in a crowd, especially when people are going in a different direction. A lot of people struggle with issues of identity and faith in a crowd.**

Pause for a few minutes, then continue: **Now think about being alone again. Only, this time, you don't want to be alone. You might picture yourself in the place you like to go to be by yourself or in a large crowd, but think about how you feel when you would rather be with friends. It's tough to be lonely and alone. It's just as hard to be lonely and in a crowd.**

After a few minutes, say: **Finally, picture individuals from this youth group. Think about some of the activities you've shared with them. Many of the people in this group are committed. They're committed to exploring their relationship with God, and their relationship with you. The friends in this group will be here for you when you're happy or sad, and you can count on that.**

Ask volunteers to describe how they felt as they imagined themselves in the different situations.

5 Small Is Beautiful

Point out that, in the past, some successful advertising campaigns have focused on the concept of "small is beautiful." In the 1960s, the Volkswagen Beetle became a best-selling car when ads poked fun at its small size and funny shape. Avis rental cars were promoted with the slogan, "We're number two. We try harder."

Challenge group members to create an ad slogan for your youth group. Brainstorm suggestions and write them on the board. Have a vote to choose the best slogan for your group.

6 Growing a Group

Bring everyone together in a circle. Reassure everyone that a group's worth does not depend on its size. You might say: **Some of you probably think that this group is too small. That doesn't mean that each of us is worth less than members of larger groups. What it says most loudly is that there are some benefits that larger groups offer that would fill some needs of people who are members of this group. Like meeting new friends. Like getting different opinions. With that in mind, what could we do to bring new people to our group?**

Pass out Student Sheet 12-B ("Who You Gonna Call?"). Give each person time to complete the worksheet. It will help group members identify friends that might like to attend your group, and to decide how they can invite them.

If time permits, ask each person to share the name of one person he or she plans to invite to the group and how each plans to offer the invitation.

Close in prayer, thanking God for each individual in your group. Ask group members to pray silently for the people named on their worksheets. Conclude by asking God to challenge the members of your group to reach out to new friends.

WHAT'S THE BEST BODY SIZE?

12-A

What's the best body size?
Look up the following passages of Scripture. What do they tell you about the size of a body of believers?

Matthew 13:31, 32 ______________________________

____

Acts 9:31 ______________________________

____

What's the best body size?
Look up the following passages of Scripture. What do they tell you about the size of a body of believers?

Mark 6:7-1 ______________________________

____

Luke 10:1-12 ______________________________

____

What's the best body size?
Look up the following passages of Scripture. What do they tell you about the size of a body of believers?

Matthew 18:20 ______________________________

____

Acts 2:40-47 ______________________________

____

What's the best body size?
Look up the following passages of Scripture. What do they tell you about the size of a body of believers?

Acts 6:1-7 ______________________________

____

Matthew 18:10-14 ______________________________

____

WHO YOU GONNA CALL?

So, the youth group's too small, huh? Well, now's your chance to do something about that. Think of all your friends and acquaintances. Who would enjoy the activities of this group? Who needs to have the same type of relationship with God that the members of this group have? Who do you know who needs this group?

Jot down the names of five friends on the blank spaces below.

If you know their phone numbers, write them in the spaces beneath the "Phone" column. If not, fill them in later.

Think about the best time and place to make each invitation. Jot that down in the "Time/Place" column.

Is there someone else in the youth group who can also invite your friend? If so, jot his or her name in the "Other Person" column. Talk to the group member at the end of this session, and ask him or her to help you invite this person.

After you've invited your friend, place a check mark (√) in the "Done" column.

NAME	*PHONE NUMBER*	*TIME/PLACE*	*OTHER PERSON*	*DONE*
______	______	______	______	❑
______	______	______	______	❑
______	______	______	______	❑
______	______	______	______	❑
______	______	______	______	❑

Session 13

People often don't say what they mean. When a kid says your group is too big, for instance, he or she might actually mean one of several things:

- "I often feel left out of the group."
- "The group is so large and rowdy that we can't accomplish anything constructive."
- "Some people get more attention than I do."
- "I want to get to know some people in the group that I don't know."

So read between the lines and discover what your group members *really* want. Look for ways to help members build new friendships. Guide kids to find places within the smaller groups that usually make up larger groups. Your kids will soon begin to enjoy the unique dynamics of a big, active group of teenagers.

"The Group Is Too Big"

Specific Aim

- To encourage kids to seek out smaller support groups within the larger group to provide more intimate fellowship; and to help them brainstorm fellowship builders that would allow them to get to know more people in the group.

Scriptural Support

- Matthew 14:15-21
- Acts 6:1-7
- Galatians 6:2

Special Preparation

- Bibles
- Copies of Student Sheet 13-A ("Growing Pains")
- Copies of Student Sheet 13-B ("A Sharing Survey")
- Pencils
- Chalkboard and chalk or newsprint and markers
- 18" strips of cloth
- A large candle

1 MINGLE MANIA

Have group members form pairs. Give each pair a strip of cloth and have one partner tie his or her right wrist to the partner's left wrist. While group members are doing this, ask them to tell their partners one important thing that happened to them during the past week.

After everyone has completed this task, each pair should be bound together by the wrists.

Announce that you will now play "Mingle Mania." First, group members should mingle in the center of the room (in bound pairs). You will call out an even number. Everyone will scramble to form a group of people that is the size of the number called. When kids form a group, they should sit down in a circle. At that point, ask each person to introduce his or her partner to the group. After group members have introduced their partners, play another round by having everyone mingle again and calling out another number. Play three or four rounds, giving everyone the chance to introduce his or her partner three or four times.

After the final round, ask everyone to untie the strips. Have a volunteer collect all of the strips of cloth and tie them together in one large, knotted rope. Save this for a later activity.

2 A SMALLER GROUP

Say: **You may not know this, but our group has been studied by the Society for Maintaining Arbitrary Legislation Leading to Education that is Restricted—SMALLER. Basically, SMALLER has been studying size differentials and quantum physics reactions to bulk, body, and boredom. It has decided that our group is just too large. Strict space deficit-reduction measures must be taken. Over the next few minutes, we will need to work together to determine how to diminish our group by 50%. We'll need to decide what criteria we'll use to reduce the group's size and how to keep a certain number of people away.**

However, since our group's problem is critical, SMALLER has decided that special measures must be taken immediately. Every minute during the discussion, some people will be "dropped" from the group. I'll announce which people are excluded every 60 seconds. Those individuals may physically remain in the room, but they cannot participate in the discussion.

Ask if there are any questions. Then begin the discussion by asking how to best "reduce your space deficit." After one minute, announce that everyone whose last name begins with the letter "A" is now out of the group. Explain that you regret this move, but those people cannot participate in the discussion. Don't let them leave the room.

After the next minute, pick a letter at random and announce that everyone whose last name begins with that letter is excluded from the group. Continue this procedure until frustration levels begin to rise (probably about five minutes). Then bring everyone together and discuss the exercise.

First, explain that *everyone* can share in the youth group activities, particularly the discussion that will follow. Naturally, no one is really excluded. There is no "Society for Maintaining Arbitrary Legislation Leading to Education that is Restricted." In fact, the idea that any church should ask someone to leave because it doesn't have room for him or her is ludicrous.

Ask those who were dropped to describe how they felt. **Was the reduction procedure fair? Was it hard to take the simulation seriously?**

Ask those who remained to describe how they felt. **Was the "smaller" group really better? What *is* better about smaller youth groups?** (It's easier to feel accepted; it's easier to get to know everyone; it's harder to get lost in the crowd.) **What's better about larger youth groups?** (They often have more variety; they generate excitement; they have more people to get to know.)

Ask: **When someone says, "This group is too large," which of the following statements are they actually making?**

(A) "I don't know some of the people here."
(B) "I feel left out of the activities and conversations of this group."
(C) "We aren't as close-knit as we used to be."
(D) "The group has a discipline problem."
(E) "The group doesn't have enough physical space."
(F) Other ______________________________

As group members offer their opinions, point out that the benefits of a large group can make it worthwhile to overcome the challenges you've been discussing. Say something like: **The early church had some problems due to rapid growth and crowds of people. Let's see how those difficulties were resolved. It might help us find answers related to our own concerns.**

3 Growing Pains

Hand out copies of Student Sheet 13-A ("Growing Pains"). Ask group members to read the Scripture passages and jot down their answers. Give them time to do so. Then lead a discussion about their findings. On the board list key words and phrases describing solutions to size problems. (One word that should come up frequently is "share." The more we share ourselves, our possessions, our time, etc., the more likely that size problems will diminish.)

Say something like: **One common theme in each situation is the necessity of sharing. How do we see that in these passages?** (When a little boy shared his fish and bread, people were fed. When the early church divided up responsibilities, people's needs were met. Paul commands us to share one another's burdens. When we do, we help and are helped by each other.)

What are some ways that you can share with others to make this group more accepting? (Suggestions might include: creating a "greeter committee"; sending welcome cards to guests; organizing "hug patrols," in which "hug police" give bearhugs to unsuspecting individuals; name tags, etc.) As individuals make suggestions, list them on the board.

4 Create a Body Builder

Divide the large group into three teams. Each team is responsible to create a "body builder"—a game or activity that will help group members get to know each other better. Encourage group members to consider their ideas carefully, because you plan to use each team's idea in future meetings. Give each team five minutes to plan. Then have each team describe its body builder to the entire group. Be sure you follow through in future meetings and lead off with these custom-made, group-building activities. Or you may want to devote an entire meeting to fellowship builders.

5 A Sharing Survey

Pass out pencils and copies of Student Sheet 13-B ("A Sharing Survey"). Each group member should identify people in the group who have demonstrated certain traits and ask those people to sign his or her survey on the appropriate line. The survey helps identify models for good sharing behavior, and it also affirms others. Give everyone time to complete his or her survey.

Say something like: **This survey shows that the real advantage to a large group is lots of people with lots to give. Let's remember to be thankful for each person in this group. We all contribute something special to make this group as great as it is.**

6 A Candlelight Worship Service

Close this session with a candlelight worship service. If the proper mood is established, this can be a very meaningful activity.

Take the long, knotted rope created earlier from 18" strips of cloth. Holding onto one end, weave throughout the room, trailing the knotted rope behind you. Ask kids to grab the rope and follow along as you pass by them. Eventually everyone should be hanging onto the rope, like a train. Swing the rope around to form a circle by catching up with the last person on the train. Ask everyone to sit on the floor in the circle, facing toward the center.

Dim the lights and place a lighted candle in front of you. If your group enjoys group singing, sing one or two favorite songs. Or you might choose to play soft music on a tape deck in the background. Ask someone to read aloud Galatians 6:2.

Explain that this is a time of sharing. You're going to pass the candle around the circle. When it is in front of a person, that person has the chance to share anything he or she wants with the group. Some may want to thank other group members for thoughtful words or deeds. Others might want to thank God for something He's done in their lives. Some may want to ask for help or prayer.

Begin the sharing process yourself, perhaps by explaining your hope or dream for this youth group. Then pass the candle to the person sitting next to you. Continue until the candle has gone around the circle.

Ask everyone to hold hands. Close in prayer. Thank God for every person who is a part of your group and ask Him to help retain the small group flavor within your large group. Invite everyone to hug four or five people before going home.

Growing Pains

Matthew 14:15-21

Jesus and the early disciples were facing size problems. Basically, the group of followers was just too large for their facilities. There wasn't enough food to feed the mob. They could have diminished the size of the group. Instead, they tried a different approach. Read Matthew 14:15-21 and see what Jesus suggested to solve this size problem.

Acts 6:1-7

The early church was facing size problems. Leaders were asked to spend too much time and energy in ministry other than preaching the Gospel. The leaders agreed that sharing funds with the needy was important, but they felt preaching the Gospel was a higher priority for them. Read Acts 6:1-7 to see how the early church dealt with this size problem.

Galatians 6:2

There are probably many reasons why Paul penned these words. As you read Galatians 6:2, think about how this might comfort people who are beginning to feel left out of a Christian group. How would it challenge people who were actively involved in a larger group?

A Sharing Survey

Think about the members of your group and their different talents and abilities. Which individuals are really good at reaching out to others? Who makes a strong effort to listen? Who is a real leader? Find these individuals, as outlined below, and ask them to sign their names beside their strengths.

Find someone who is a real leader. The group listens and follows when this person says, "Go!" Tell him or her to "keep up the good work." Then ask him or her to sign here:

____

Find someone who is a great listener. You always feel like you can talk to this person. Ask him or her to sign here: ____________________

Find someone who always reaches out to newcomers. Nobody is just a guest when this person's around. Everyone feels right at home. Ask him or her to sign here:

____

Find someone who is the ideal "Idea Person." Clever. Resourceful. A great problem solver. Give him or her a "pat on the back," then ask him or her to sign here:

____

Find someone who is a lot of fun to be around. This person always keeps them "rolling in the aisles." Ask him or her to tell you a joke, then sign here: ____________________

Find someone who always seems to notice when you're feeling down. This person is extremely empathetic. Give him or her a big hug, then ask him or her to sign here:

____

Find someone who always shares a smile, regardless of the situation. You can always count on him or her to brighten your day. Smile, then ask him or her to sign here:

____

Find someone who is always working hard for this youth group. This person seems to have an endless well of energy when it comes to the group. Say, "Thanks for everything," then ask him or her to sign here: ____________________

Session 14

It seems like Larry never takes his hands out of his letter jacket pockets. He leans back in his chair and silently challenges you to get him to laugh, answer a question, or be more than just half-hearted about his participation. Larry has told you that he only attends because he *has* to. His parents insist. And that makes Larry want to resist your efforts to interest him.

You can reach the Larrys in your group. But first you need to help them understand that they are free to make their own choices about their spiritual growth. And you need to encourage them to use that freedom to build a faith that belongs to them—not their parents. This session can help group members like Larry consider their parents' perspective and think more objectively about their own church participation.

"I Just Come Because My Parents Make Me"

Specific Aim

- To help kids understand the importance of establishing their own faith apart from their parents; and to help them see how hostility and apathy affect the whole group.

Scriptural Support

- Ephesians 6:1-3
- Colossians 3:20

Special Preparation

- Bibles
- Copies of Student Sheet 14-A ("A House of Cards")
- Copies of Student Sheet 14-B ("What Do You Think They Think?")
- Pencils
- Envelopes
- Paper
- Index cards

1 Parent Poll

Read aloud the following statements. Ask group members to vote on each by giving a "thumbs up" sign if they agree or a "thumbs down" sign if they disagree. If they "intensely agree," ask them to raise their thumbs in the air. If they "intensely disagree," ask them to hold their thumbs low to the floor.

- **My parents make me do household chores.**
- **My parents make me babysit my little brother or sister.**
- **My parents make me attend "family" activities.**
- **My parents make me go to church.**
- **My parents make me come to youth group.**
- **My parents make me study every night.**
- **My parents keep me from watching certain TV shows.**
- **My parents make me eat healthy food.**
- **My parents are strict.**

2 Parent Potential

Divide into small groups. Have each person write his or her name on an index card and place it in the center of the small group. Ask one person to collect the cards, shuffle them, and pass them out again. No one should know who has his or her card.

During the next few minutes, you'll ask several questions. Each group member should tell the small group how he or she thinks the person whose card he or she has would respond. Wild guessing is allowed if kids don't know each other well. (Be sure to pause after each question so group members can share their answers with their groups.)

Ten years from now, if this person is a parent . . .

- **Will he let his son or daughter talk him into staying up 30 minutes later to watch a favorite TV show?**
- **Will she let her son or daughter nibble on cookies before dinner?**
- **Will he spoil his son or daughter at Christmas?**
- **Will she make her son or daughter go to Sunday school?**
- **Will he let his ten year old stay up all night when a friend stays overnight?**
- **Will she make her son or daughter study a certain number of hours each night?**
- **Will he encourage his son or daughter to take piano lessons?**

Twenty years from now, if this person is an older parent . . .

- **Will he buy his son or daughter a car?**
- **Will she buy her son or daughter a brand-new car?**
- **Will he let his son or daughter date at age 13? age 12? age 11?**
- **Will she encourage her son or daughter to attend school dances?**
- **Will he let his 16 year old stay at home over the weekend by himself?**

- **Will she make her son or daughter attend youth group?**
- **Will he encourage his son or daughter to get a job?**

On a scale of 1-10—1 being "lenient" and 10 being "strict"—how strict will this person be?

After the questions have been answered, ask group members to tell whose name they had. Then have them share their responses. Ask: **Were the answers accurate?**

Was anyone surprised by the perceptions others had of them?

Do you think you will be a strict or lenient parent? Why?

In what ways can strictness be good for you? How can it be negative?

3 A Challenge to Obedience

Ask: **What should your response be to a strict parent?** (Obedience, if the parent doesn't cause you mental or physical harm.)

How should you respond when your parents makes you come to the youth group? (Consider that they might have a good reason for asking you to be involved in the youth group and look for positive things about the group.)

Ask two volunteers to read aloud Ephesians 6:1-3 and Colossians 3:20. Ask: **What do these passages say about obeying your parents?** (These passages instruct children to obey their parents.) **What should someone do if his or her parents require attending the youth group?** (He or she should attend the group out of obedience.)

Say something like: **Someone once said, "It's not true because it's in the Bible. It's in the Bible because it's true!" That's a way of saying that the Bible makes good sense. Give three good reasons why children should obey their parents.** (Parents have the benefit of experience; parents generally love their children and are usually looking out for them.)

Give three (or more) good reasons why you should obey your parents when they tell you to attend church or youth group. (They want us to learn about God; they trust the leaders of the youth program; they think it would be fun.)

Let's look at it from another point of view. What's the worst thing that can happen if you participate in the youth group? (Kids may offer several answers. The most popular will probably be that it will be a waste of time.)

What might be the best thing that can happen if you participate in this youth group? (Your kids might say: I might become a Christian; I might enjoy myself; I might have fun; I could learn something.)

4 A Building Exercise

Form the same groups you did at the beginning of this session. Place a stack of blank index cards in the center of each group. Pass out the assignment cards from Student Sheet 14-A ("A House of Cards"). Make sure that one person in each group gets the "Cynic" card.

Challenge each group to try to build the tallest house of cards out of the index cards. However, each person must follow the instructions on his or her assignment card and must keep his or her role a secret. Only those who have "Builder" cards can actually touch the index cards. Those with "Voice" cards can make verbal suggestions. Those with "Observer" cards can only watch what happens. The "Cynic" card holders can make verbal suggestions, but they should be as negative as they can. Give group members about five minutes to build their card houses.

Ask the Observer to tell what happened in his or her group. Ask others to add to his or her observations. Most will probably report that the Cynic was divisive and unproductive.

Ask: **How can a negative attitude bring down our group?** (Negativity can be depressing. It often makes people feel defensive.) **What can you do to combat feelings of apathy and hostility when your parents make you attend the youth group?** (Try to look on the positive side; try to take a different perspective.)

Does it help to know that parents who make their kids attend this group probably want the best for their kids?

5 See the Similarities

Say: **Have you ever wondered how different you really are from your parents? Maybe this worksheet can help you find out.** Pass out copies of Student Sheet 14-B ("What Do You Think They Think?"). This survey is designed to compare each young person's views and values with those of his or her parents. Group members will mark those statements they agree with by placing a check in the left-hand column. They will then mark the statements they believe their parents agree with in the column on the right.

Ask: **How similar are your answers to those that you thought your parents might give? What differences do you think exist between your views and those of your parents?**

Ask for volunteers who were born between January 1 and June 30 to tell how similar answers between parents and their kids can be healthy. (It could be a sign of harmony and agreement between kids and their parents; it may show that parents and kids have discussed the values and have come to similar agreements.)

Ask everyone who was born between July 1 and December 31 to share how dissimilar answers might be positive. (It could be a sign of independent thought; it could indicate that parents and kids encourage and allow each other to stretch one another's thinking.)

Encourage everyone to take his or her worksheet home, tear off the bottom, and ask one of his or her parents to complete the survey. Later, group members can compare their answers and their projected parents' answers with their parents' actual answers. The results may be quite interesting.

6 Take a Letter

Ask: **What do your parents do to make it easy for you to attend this youth group? Do they really know what you do in this youth group? If your parents make you come to this group, why do you think they do?**

Pass out blank sheets of paper, envelopes, and pencils to each person. Ask group members to write their own letters about the youth group to their parents. They may want to explain what they do in the group. They might want to describe how they feel about the things their parents do to make it possible for them to participate in your group. They may want to thank their parents for their support.

After everyone has finished, ask if volunteers would like to share their letters with the group. (You might want to model this by reading a similar letter you've written to a friend or spouse.) Invite group members to seal their letters in the blank envelopes and to deliver them to their parents.

Close in prayer, thanking God for parents who care enough to guide their children to go to church. Ask God to help your group members find ways to cooperate with their parents.

A House of Cards

Builder

Your job is to stack the cards on top of each other to build as tall a stack of cards as you can. You cannot talk to anyone in your group.

Voice

You can talk to anyone in the group that you want to. Feel free to make suggestions and offer advice. You cannot touch the cards.

Observer

You cannot talk to anyone in the group. Neither can you handle the cards. You can only watch what takes place for comment later.

Cynic

You cannot touch the cards in your group. But you can talk. Your job is to be as negative as you can. Try to discourage the group by pointing out errors and spreading doubts.

What Do You Think They Think?

14-B

Indicate your beliefs in the column on the left. Check the ones you agree with and leave the ones you disagree with blank. Then think about one of your parents. Would he or she agree with the statements? If so, check the columns on the right. When you get home, give that parent the bottom half of this survey. Then compare your answers (and your projected answers) with your parent's answers.

I Agree	***Statement***	***My Parent Would Agree***
❑	I think our country should spend more on national defense.	❑
❑	I think our country should do more to help the homeless.	❑
❑	I think our country should do more to help senior citizens.	❑
❑	Sometimes I just don't feel good about myself.	❑
❑	Sometimes I worry about the way I look.	❑
❑	Sometimes I worry about how my friends treat me.	❑
❑	Sometimes I have doubts about my spiritual beliefs.	❑
❑	I believe the Bible is God's inspired Word.	❑
❑	My faith is the most important thing in my life.	❑
❑	I enjoy going to church every week.	❑
❑	I wish I knew more about the Bible.	❑
❑	I believe that Jesus is the Son of God.	❑
❑	There are long periods of time during which I never pray.	❑
❑	I wish I could pray more effectively.	❑
❑	Drug/alcohol abuse is a big problem in our community.	❑
❑	I believe parents shouldn't force their kids to do things that the kids don't want to do.	❑

Please complete the following survey for our youth group.

I Agree	***Statement***
❑	I think our country should spend more on national defense.
❑	I think our country should do more to help the homeless.
❑	I think our country should do more to help senior citizens.
❑	Sometimes I just don't feel good about myself.
❑	Sometimes I worry about the way I look.
❑	Sometimes I worry about how my friends treat me.
❑	Sometimes I have doubts about my spiritual beliefs.
❑	I believe the Bible is God's inspired Word.
❑	My faith is the most important thing in my life.
❑	I enjoy going to church every week.
❑	I wish I knew more about the Bible.
❑	I believe that Jesus is the Son of God.
❑	There are long spells during which I never pray.
❑	I wish I could pray more effectively.
❑	Drug/alcohol abuse is a big problem in our community.
❑	I believe parents shouldn't force their kids to do things that the kids don't want to do.

Session 15

Most kids question their belief in God at one time or another. When it happens in the middle of your youth group meeting or Sunday school class, it can be a little threatening. But we need to encourage kids to express their honest doubts instead of hiding them away.

Doubt can cause your young people to search for answers. In fact, doubt can actually bring kids closer to God as they begin to own their faith. So we need to reassure them that it's OK to ask tough questions. And we also need to offer kids answers that make sense as they struggle to understand. Let doubt be the catalyst in your group to spark a challenging time of spiritual growth.

"I'm Not Sure I Believe in God Anymore"

Specific Aim

• To help kids understand that there is nothing wrong with doubting—it's natural, and it's a sign of a probing mind; to help them recognize their continued acceptance by the group; to help them recognize evidences of God and His handiwork throughout nature; and to help them understand the hopelessness of a world without God.

Scriptural Support

- Psalm 19:1-6
- John 20:24-29
- Acts 14:8-18; 17:24-28
- Romans 1:18-20

Special Preparation

- Bibles
- Copies of Student Sheet 15-A ("I Doubt It")
- Copies of Student Sheet 15-B ("A Reason to Believe")
- Pencils
- Chalkboard and chalk or newsprint and marker
- Index cards

1 I Doubt It

Say something like: **Let's see a show of hands. How many people in this room believe everything they hear on the radio? How many believe everything they read in the newspapers or magazines? How many believe everything they hear on *Entertainment Tonight*? How many believe everything their parents tell them? How many believe everything their friends say?**

No doubt, some of you have doubts about a few things you see and hear. Here's a self-test to help define a few of those doubts.

Distribute copies of Student Sheet 15-A ("I Doubt It"). Group members should read through the list and place a check next to each statement they doubt.

After they have finished, ask them to go back and underline those statements which are probably doubted by most of the people in this country. Then ask them to circle those statements that would be doubted by the majority of their friends. Finally, ask them to draw a line through those statements likely to be doubted by most people in your church.

Ask: **Were there any statements left which only you doubt?** Explain that we all have doubts, and many of them are shared by others in our lives. The difficulty occurs when we feel our doubts come into conflict with the beliefs of those close to us. As a result, we may want to hide our honest feelings and questions.

Say something like: **Someone once said, "Doubt is the growing edge of faith." How can doubt cause spiritual growth?** (When people face up to honest doubts, they can be motivated to find answers.)

How can doubts be destructive to one's faith? (If people don't look for answers to their questions, their doubts can make them stop believing.)

Is it good or bad to have doubts about God and Christianity? (It can be good because it is the sign of a probing mind. Not only can it be good, but it is natural. Most people face doubts about their beliefs.)

2 A World-Class Doubter

Ask a volunteer to read John 20:24-29. (This event lends itself to dramatization, so if you have some enthusiastic performers, you may want to ask them ahead of time to prepare a dramatic reading of the passage.)

Say something like: **The Bible is full of examples of people who have doubts about God and His promises. We've just heard about the most famous doubter of them all: Doubting Thomas. What kind of proof did Thomas require of Jesus?** (He needed to see and touch the evidence of a resurrected Christ. He wanted to see and feel the nail imprints and touch Jesus' side, which had been pierced.)

How did Jesus react to Thomas' request? (He offered the concrete proof that Thomas wanted.)

Point out that Jesus did not reject Thomas because of the disciple's doubts. He responded in love to meet Thomas' need for more proof. Perhaps because that loving response was so characteristic of Jesus, Thomas recognized Him as "my Lord and my God."

Say: **Most of us can relate to Thomas because we often doubt what we can't see or feel. In addition to the fact that we can't see or touch Him, what other reasons might we have for doubting the reality of God?** List responses on the board.

Some possibilities might include:

- Some see hypocrisy in the church and find it hard to believe that real faith could exist with so much false behavior.
- Some people feel God has broken His promises or failed to meet their expectations. How can He exist when He never answers their prayers?
- Some people think God is for little kids in Sunday school or adults who want everything neat and tidy. Their friends don't believe in God, so why should they?

Encourage group members to be honest and thoughtful in their responses.

Say: **There are many different reasons for doubt. But there are also some good reasons to believe. God has chosen to reveal Himself to us through Jesus Christ and through His Word. Let's look to Scripture for some reasonable arguments for faith.**

3 GIVE ME ONE GOOD REASON

Divide your group into four teams. Give each team a discussion guide from Student Sheet 15-B ("A Reason to Believe"). If your group is large, you may want to make more copies of the guides and have eight teams. Each team should read the Scripture passages listed, discuss the questions, and report its answers to the entire group afterward.

You may want to supplement their reports with the following points.

Team 1 (Psalm 19:1-6)—Creation is so amazing that even without words, the sky, sun, moon, and stars reveal the existence of a divine Creator. His message is available to everyone on earth. Even those who lack the Bible have been moved to ask, "Who made the sun?"

Team 2 (Acts 14:8-18)—Paul and Barnabas tried to convince their listeners to turn to the one true and living God. He is recognizable not only from His creating rain and crops, but also by the good gifts He gives—such as food and joy.

Team 3 (Acts 17:24-28)—God revealed Himself in creation and history so that people would seek Him. We are His children—created in His image—so we should be asking questions about our Creator.

Team 4 (Romans 1:18-20)—The variety and miracles of nature reveal a God who is alive, creative, vital, loving, humorous, and above all, seeking a relationship with His creation: people.

In summary, be sure to stress that there are clear evidences of God's presence through His creation. Those things point the way to God, but it is up to us individually to respond in trust and faith.

4 Too Good Not to Be True

Point out that some things in life seem so incredible and amazing that it is easy to believe an intelligent mind is behind it all. Mention wonders of nature or situations in life that have affected you this way (the beauty and majesty of a specific natural wonder; the miracle of a newborn baby; the complexity of the human body, etc.). Ask group members to offer their own examples. List these on the board.

Ask: **If we can see God's hand at work in the world, can we also imagine what the world would be like without God? What changes might we see in people and the world if God didn't exist?** (Since God is the Creator, people and the world wouldn't even exist; without God we would have no model for love or compassion; without God, all would be chaos, etc.) List group members' ideas on the board.

Point out that if we did have a world independent of a loving God, it would not likely be a place in which we would want to live.

5 A Talk with the Creator

Say something like: **Since we are made in God's image, we have the ability to think creatively and intelligently. This gives us the ability to ask questions and doubt. God is probably pleased when we exercise our minds and ask those tough questions. But we shouldn't be asking them in a vacuum. We can go to Him and ask for help in resolving our doubts.**

Distribute index cards, one to a person. Ask each group member to write at least one doubt or tough question on his or her card. Then have group members fold their cards and hold onto them during a time of prayer.

As you lead the group in a closing prayer, include time for group members to silently address God about their doubts and questions. Encourage them to be honest with their Creator about these difficult feelings and thoughts with which they may be struggling.

Afterward, encourage your kids to keep their cards in their Bibles or elsewhere for six months to a year. Challenge them to keep asking God for His answers during that time. When they review their cards in the future, they may discover some of their doubts fading away as they learn more and their relationships with God grow stronger.

I Doubt It

Look over this list of statements and place a check mark next to those you doubt are true.

___ The world is millions of years old.

___ God made the world.

___ Jesus is the Son of God.

___ Jesus is the only way to heaven.

___ School is easy.

___ School is fun.

___ School is necessary to succeed in life.

___ There is life on other planets.

___ People from earth will someday live on other planets.

___ Pee-wee Herman came from another planet.

___ The Bible is God's Word.

___ People who reject God will end up in hell.

___ I will be rich one day.

___ I will be famous one day.

___ I will end up in jail one day.

___ It's a sin to listen to rock music.

___ It's a sin to listen to country music.

___ It's a sin to listen to rap music.

___ It's a sin to listen to any music written after the year 1834.

A Reason to Believe

Team 1—Read Psalm 19:1-6 and discuss the following:

1. How do the heavens tell of the glory of God?

2. How is it possible to know about God without the use of words?

3. If you knew nothing of God or the Bible, would you wonder who made the sun? Why or why not?

4. Do you believe the message of God's existence has gone out through *all* the earth? Why or why not?

Team 2—Read Acts 14:8-18 and discuss the following:

1. How did Barnabas and Paul react when the crowd wanted to worship them? Why did they react that way?

2. What evidence do they offer of a living God?

3. Does their argument make sense to you? Why or why not?

4. How successful were they in convincing the crowd that they weren't gods?

Team 3 —Read Acts 17:24-28 and discuss the following:

1. What did God do to encourage people to seek and find Him?

2. How should being God's offspring (children) help us to know and understand God?

3. How do our human limitations restrict our understanding of God?

Team 4 —Read Romans 1:18-20 and discuss the following:

1. Paul says knowledge concerning God is available to all. How has God made Himself plain (or visible) to people?

2. How does creation reveal God to us?

3. What qualities of God can be discovered through creation?

4. Do you think people have no excuse for not believing in God? Why or why not?